Bu
London

THE OFFICIAL LONDON TRANSPORT GUIDE TO EXPLORING LONDON ON A SHOESTRING

LONDON TRANSPORT

Published jointly by **London Transport, 55 Broadway, Westminster, London SW1** and **Book Production Consultants, 47 Norfolk Street, Cambridge CB1 2LE**

Published 1991.
© London Transport and Book Production Consultants 1991.
ISBN 1 871829 06 2

A CIP catalogue record for this book is available from the British Library.

Enquiries regarding advertising in future editions of this and other guides in the series should be addressed to **Book Production Consultants, 47 Norfolk Street, Cambridge CB1 2LE.**

Other Guides in the series:
Family London
London Breaks
Royal & Historic London

The publishers would like to thank the following for their permission to reproduce photographs: pp.14 (left), 16, 18 (both), 20, 22, 35, 36, 37, 43, 58, 60, 61, 74 (bottom), 75 (bottom), 77 (top), 97 (bottom), 98, 99 (top), 100 (top left), J C Mervyn Blatch; p.14 (bottom), House of Commons Public Information Office; pp.15, 32, 74 (top), 77 (bottom), 83, 115, David Phillips; p.17, Imperial War Museum; pp.19, 56, 57, 97 (top and middle), Crown copyright and reproduced with the permission of the controller of HMSO; p.21, Liberty Retail Limited; p.34 (top), London Transport Museum; p.34 (bottom), Woodmansterne Picture Library; p.59 (top), Imperial War Museum; pp.59 (bottom), 99 (bottom), London Docklands Development Corporation; pp.63, 64, Museum of the Moving Image; p.75 (top), National Portrait Gallery; p.78, The London Tourist Board; pp.80, 82 (top), By courtesy of the Board of Trustees of the Victoria & Albert Museum; p.81, Harrods Limited; p.82 (bottom), The National History Museum; p.84, The Royal Albert Hall; p.100 (top right and bottom), National Maritime Museum.

Design and production by **Book Production Consultants**

Based on *Free (or nearly free) London*, originally published by London Transport. Text completely revised and updated by **Jenny Ward**.

Cover design by **Peter Dolton**
Book design by **Jim Reader**
Illustrations by **John York**
Maps by **FWT, London N19**
Film origination by **Anglia Graphics, Bedford**
Printed and bound in the United Kingdom by **Staples Printers (Kettering) Ltd.**

CONTENTS

INTRODUCTION

Ships, towers, domes, theatres, and temples lie
Open unto the fields, and to the sky;

wrote Wordsworth on a visit to London
one day in September 1802. Nearly two hundred
years later the skyline displays shapes he would not be
able to identify, but many of the things he did see remain.
There are even traces of the fields he glimpsed from
Westminster Bridge in place-names such as Lincoln's Inn
Fields. London is ever changing, but one thing that does
not change is the abundance of things to see
and enjoy that it offers to visitors.

The four official London Transport guides – *Royal &
Historic London, Budget London, Family London* and
London Breaks – are designed for the visitor to London
who has little time to spare. To get the most out of a short
stay or day trip, choose the book that best suits your
pocket and your needs. *Royal & Historic London* is the
one for those who particularly want to see the traditional
places and events. *Budget London* has lots of suggestions
for enjoying yourself with the minimum outlay; it takes in
all the major tourist attractions in doing that. *Family
London* offers ideas for all ages – and if your group includes someone who is disabled, note that the walks in it
contain specific information for wheelchair users. All the
guides include a Disabled in London section with transport advice.

These tours were originally devised by London jour-
nalist Keith Blogg in the early 1980s and since then they
have been tried and tested by eight million visitors. They
have been completely checked and re-written to bring
them up to date for the 1990s. Each walk can be
completed in a day, with some help here and there from
buses and tubes. Follow all four walks in the guide and
you will be sure of seeing all the main features that central
London has to offer. If you prefer to plan your own route,
you will find that the walks are interconnected and that it
is easy for you to switch back and forth between them as
you wish.

What made London great, from Roman times onwards, was its main highway, the Thames. It's no coincidence that most of the sights of London are close to it. The Thames has been coming into its own again in recent years with the development of Docklands. You may like to use the river as a highway in your explorations in the city, or you can mix a river and coach trip to see further afield. Turn to the side trips for ideas.

A brief guide to the ever-changing nightlife of London is included in a separate section. You can experience the atmosphere of London after dark by simply exploring the streets mentioned. If you want to do more than that, you will need up-to-the-minute information to supplement what is given here. Consult the daily papers and specialist weeklies such as *Time Out, City Limits* and *What's On.*

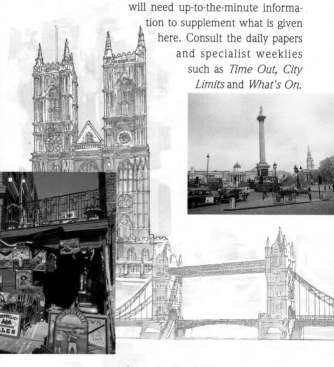

To help you find your way, there is a map for each walk showing the route and the places of interest described. At the end of the guide there is a pull-out map giving you a comprehensive view of the capital city. There are so many things to see in a short distance in central London that sometimes there is too much detail to be shown clearly in the space available on the maps. You will find it useful to have a copy of a detailed plan such as the *London A to Z* to consult alongside the ones supplied here.

Along the top of each of the double-page spreads to the walks, you will find a simplified linear representation of the instructions provided in the text beneath. Be sure to refer to the text and map for directions.

Entrance information is given at the end of each walk, together with phone numbers. It is wise to check a day or so in advance that your main destinations will be open when you plan to visit, especially as sometimes special events can disrupt public access. Opening times and prices are always changing and the details given should be used for general guidance only. For tourist information in office hours the London Tourist Board has a helpline on 071-730 3488.

You may prefer to travel by public transport rather than to walk between the places you visit. If so, make use of the details given about buses and tube stations at the end of each walk. Cafes and toilets are mentioned occasionally where they are thin on the ground, but you will not have any problem in finding these in the centre.

Travel information cannot be guaranteed in advance as London Transport is continually improving routes and services. For travel enquiries dial London Transport on 071-222 1234, or Travelcheck (for recorded, up-to-the-minute information) on 071-222 1200. If you are dialling from a number with the same prefix as the one you need, leave out the prefix. Each of these numbers has a queuing system; if you re-dial you lose your place, so hang on if you don't get a reply at first. There are separate sections towards the end of the guide with more detailed transport and tourist information.

Above all, enjoy your stay, and welcome to London.

KEY

U   Nearest Underground station

BR   Nearest British Rail station

DLR   Nearest Docklands Light Railway station

D   Access for the disabled

CABINET WAR
ROOMS

VISIT THE
NERVE CENTRE
OF BRITAIN'S
WAR EFFORT

OPEN DAILY
⊖ WESTMINSTER
CABINET WAR ROOMS
CLIVE STEPS, KING CHARLES STREET,
LONDON SWIA 2AQ 01-930 6961

Bank *of* England Museum
Bartholomew Lane EC2

Open Mon - Fri 10.00-17.00 all year.
Sun and Bank Hols 11.00-1700
from 29/3 to 29/9.

Admission Free
071 601 5545

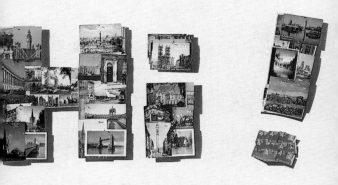

While you're seeing the sights in Britain don't forget the folks back home. In any language a postcard is the brightest, quickest and simplest way to say Hi!

They take seconds to write and arrive at their destination in no time at all. They are also great value.

Stamps are available in handy books of four which you can carry with you wherever you travel.

Pick up a book from post offices or anywhere you see the Royal Mail Stockist signs.

P.S. *Want to say more? Or say it more personally? Then send a colourful new pictorial aerogramme, available from post offices.*

Royal Mail

International

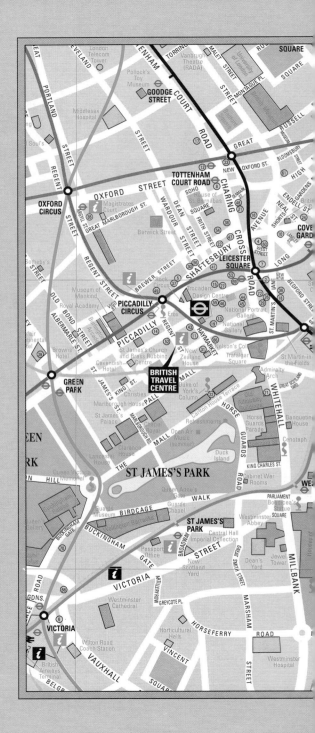

WALK 1

SCOTLAND YARD
WESTMINSTER ABBEY
PARLIAMENT
DOWNING STREET
PICCADILLY CIRCUS
CARNABY STREET
BRITISH MUSEUM

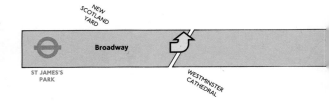

Broadway

ST JAMES'S PARK

WESTMINSTER CATHEDRAL

S t James's Park Underground station is not a historic monument, but situated in the basement of London Transport's headquarters at 55 Broadway it is definitely more palatial than LT's other tube stations. Outside, to your right, round the arcade of shops and past LT's Travel Shop (see Using London's Public Transport section for more details), is the solemnly revolving sign of **New Scotland Yard**, home of the Metropolitan Police since 1967. You will see old New Scotland Yard a little later on. Walk to the corner of Victoria Street and look to your right. You may be able to see the Byzantine campanile of **Westminster Cathedral**, the mother church in England of Roman Catholics, which has a fine viewing gallery at the top. To your left is **Westminster Abbey**, now revealed by cleaning as white enough to star in a toothpaste advertisement. It was founded by Edward the Confessor in 1065 and was rebuilt in Early English Gothic under Henry III. However, the exterior is mostly nineteenth-century Gothic.

Westminster Abbey

WESTMINSTER ABBEY

Entry is free, but once inside the inevitable outstretched palm makes an added expense of a pilgrimage to Poets' Corner or a communing with the early kings and queens of England, including Edward himself. The Coronation Chair with the Scots' Coronation Stone, or Stone of Scone, beneath it is behind the barrier

Westminster Cathedral

too. A charge is also made for the Pyx Chamber (now a treasury), the Chapter House (home of Parliament in the fourteenth century) and the Undercroft Museum. These are found together in the cloisters by leaving the main building near Poets' Corner. In the museum are wax effigies – of monarchs and other notables – that started out as funeral items. The effigy would lie above the mortal remains in the funeral procession. The oldest is the wooden figure of Edward III, which reveals that he had suffered a stroke. The head of Henry VII, moulded from a death mask, shows an authoritative, calculating face, surprisingly modern. The Duchess of Richmond, an early mistress of Charles II, is shown with her stuffed parrot, an ancient deceased bird. The Duchess, quite a beauty in her day, was thrown over in favour of Nell Gwyn. The merry

The Jewel Tower

monarch kept at least three mistresses at any one time, plus a resigned queen and a resident procuress. The best time to visit Westminster Abbey is on Wednesdays between 6 and 7.45 when not only is the whole abbey free of charge but amateur photography is allowed. There are times, however, when the abbey is closed for state occasions and other church services.

ST MARGARET'S WESTMINSTER

In the abbey grounds pause at **St Margaret's church**, the parish church of the House of Commons. William Caxton, the father of English printing, is remembered on a wall plaque and most of Sir Walter Raleigh is buried here (his

St Margaret Street

St Margaret Street

JEWEL TOWER

HOUSES OF PARLIAMENT

BIG BEN

head is elsewhere). Coming out of St Margaret's opposite Parliament, turn right for a quick peep at the **Jewel Tower**, part of the mediaeval Palace of Westminster and once a royal treasury. The ground floor is free though there is nothing here of interest but the building itself. Across the road are the ornate **Houses of Parliament**, built in the last century after fire ravaged the earlier building, the one where Guy Fawkes was left guarding the gunpowder in 1605. Explosives have become easier to hide since then and the buildings are not open to the public for security reasons, though your MP can invite you in.

ALONG THE EMBANKMENT

Cross the road and turn left towards **Big Ben**, passing the statues of Richard the

Big Ben

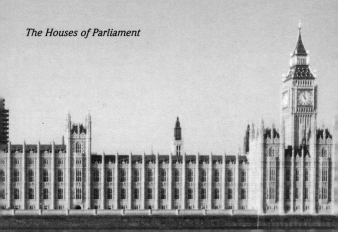

The Houses of Parliament

OLD NEW
SCOTLAND
YARD

St Margaret Street — **Bridge Street**

Lionheart and Cromwell on your right and Churchill on your left. Big Ben was originally the nickname of the bell inside the clock tower, named after Sir Benjamin Hall, Commissioner of Works when the Great Clock was raised in 1856. When Parliament

Statue of Boadicea

is sitting a light shines in the clock tower.

Turn right towards Westminster Bridge. On the embankment above the public conveniences is Thornycroft's statue of Boadicea, Queen of the Iceni, in her knife-wheeled chariot. She gave the Romans a bad time in 61 AD. They returned the favour and she is reputed to be

buried under platform 9 at King's Cross station. The building with the horizontal stripes facing the river is old **New Scotland Yard**, home of the Metropolitan Police from 1890 to 1967, beloved of film makers. It is referred to as the 'Norman Shaw building' after its Victorian architect. The granite for it was quarried, appropriately, by Dartmoor convicts. The turret office overlooking the river was the Commissioner's. In

Old New Scotland Yard

1891 the Metropolitan

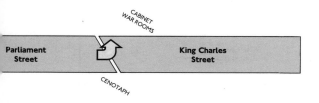

Police's lost property office here handled 14,212 umbrellas, 4 sets of dentures and a stuffed badger. (The original headquarters of the Met, from 1829, was in Great Scotland Yard, at the other end of Whitehall.)

REMEMBERING THE WAR

Now turn down Parliament Street, which later becomes Whitehall. In the centre of the traffic stands the **Cenotaph**, the nation's monument to the dead of two world wars. The word 'cenotaph' means empty tomb. It is almost opposite a triple archway which leads to King Charles Street and government offices. At the far end of the street are the **Cabinet War Rooms**, the underground suite of rooms used by Churchill and the Cabinet during the war, with its map room where the progress of the war was plotted with lengths of coloured wool and pins, and where Churchill talked to President Roosevelt on the first hotline. It is pretty much as it was when it was closed in August 1945 and the cassette given in exchange for the entry fee re-creates the wartime atmosphere with chilling effectiveness via the intimate medium of headphones as

The Cabinet War Rooms

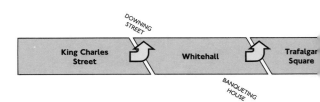

you walk around. If you can afford to spend entry money on one item per day, this gives top value. They could do with some more chairs, though. The entrance is by Clive Steps at the other end of the street. The steps look out over **St James's Park** and **Duck Island**, a nature

St James's Park

reserve not open to the public. To your right can be seen **Horse Guards Parade** where the Queen troops the colour on her official birthday in June to the accompaniment of the massed bands of the Brigade of Guards.

WHITEHALL

Walk back up King Charles Street to Whitehall and turn left towards Trafalgar Square. **Downing Street** is the next turning, now permanently gated and patrolled as here live the

Horse Guards Parade

Prime Minister, at Number 10, and the Chancellor of the Exchequer, at Number 11. Soon the other side of Horse Guards Parade is reached. A colourful guard-changing ceremony takes place here daily at 11. The guards are immobile and unresponsive according to their training, but the horses are friendly and trusting.

Across Whitehall is the **Banqueting House** of the old Whitehall Palace. (Whitehall was once a private road through the palace.) It was completed by Inigo Jones in

Cockspur Street

Pall Mall

Banqueting House

1623 as part of a plan to rebuild the whole palace but the money ran out. Charles I was beheaded outside the building in January 1649. At his restoration Charles II had his Court here, conveniently close to Drury Lane theatre. Restoration Court life was centred on this area – or at least the nightlife was – and Charles himself could be seen criss-crossing the area in pursuit of (the fair) sex. Pepys saw him as far afield as Somerset House, the Richmonds' home, climbing over the wall at night.

MAKING HAY

Now you are crossing the route of Walk 4, but today skirt around the side of Trafalgar Square, past Admiralty Arch, and into **Pall Mall**, which is named after a ball game something like croquet. Charles set up Nell Gwyn at 79 Pall Mall, where (her biographer tells us) she caught her coachman fighting with a neighbour's footman. She called out of a first-floor window to ask them to stop. The coachman called up: 'He called you a whore Mrs Nelly!' She answered: 'Well, I am a whore, find something better to fight about.' The reply came: 'You may not take it ill to be called a whore, but I will

not be called a whore's coachman.'

The area stayed bawdily disreputable even after John Nash reconstructed Pall Mall and much of this area for the Prince Regent 150 years later. **Haymarket** was originally used as its name suggests, for dealing in hay, but Nash had gentrified it by 1821, when he completed the **Theatre Royal**. At the top of the street on the right is the **Design Centre**, a free exhibition centre devoted to innovations in design, and ahead is **Piccadilly Circus**, the hub of the old empire.

St James's church, Piccadilly

PICCADILLY CIRCUS

The statue of the Angel of Christian Charity – or Eros, as he is more often called – no longer stands marooned on a traffic island. He has been shifted to the pavement, apparently so that people can use his steps as a rendezvous. Piccadilly is now geared to the young. Opposite the top of Haymarket is the London Pavilion, the home of shops and **Rock Circus**, an animated musical display put on by Madame Tussaud's. Next to it is the **Trocadero**, a place for the lively 11-year-old. It has shiny lights reflected in mirrors, music, noise, things to ride on, buttons to push, the Guinness World of Records and a Beatles exhibition. Although there are charges for Rock Circus and the exhibitions in the Trocadero, there is plenty to see for free.

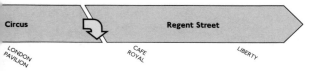

Circus

LONDON PAVILION

Regent Street

CAFE ROYAL

LIBERTY

PICCADILLY

Stretching west is **Piccadilly** itself and just a minute or two's detour takes you to **St James's church** which has a wholefood cafe and a visitors' centre offering help and advice. On Fridays and Saturdays there is an art and craft market in its grounds. A little further down is **Fortnum and Mason's** for sumptuous window-shopping. Purchase of a small item will furnish you with a Fortnum's carrier bag bearing a picture of the famous clock. Outside above the door Mr Fortnum and Mr Mason come out and bow to each other as the hours chime. **Burlington Arcade** across the road was built in 1819 and is lined with tiny shops, selling expensive and easily transportable gifts. The arcade leads to the **Museum of Mankind**, an arm of the British Museum, with anthropological exhibits from all over the world.

REGENT STREET

Returning to Piccadilly Circus, turn left up Regent Street, the curved highway created through London for the Prince Regent – again by John Nash, though his frontages have been ruined by a later generation. On the right is the **Café Royal**, haunt of Bohemian Londoners like Oscar Wilde, Bernard Shaw and Whistler at the turn of the century.

A stroll up Regent Street reveals many interesting shops and department stores to browse around: Garrard

Liberty, Regent Street

(the Crown jewellers), the Japanese Shop, Austin Reed, Hamleys – the world's largest toy shop (on five floors) – and Liberty, constructed in part from old ship timbers.

Turn right at Liberty into the now pedestrianised Great Marlborough Street. Monopoly players will see orange here and should connect Marlborough Street, Vine Street and Bow Street together as police stations. Marlborough Street magistrates' court, serving the West End, was where the Profumo/Christine Keeler case burst into the news in the 1960s and if the sixties 'swung', this was the corner where it was all happening. Carnaby Street (parallel to Regent Street) is still swinging in the nineties – or trying to. Take a break at the Shakespeare's Head pub.

TYBURN ROAD

Turn up Argyll Street opposite the back entrance of Liberty to Oxford Circus tube station if you wish to break here for today. The next destination is the **British Museum**. The

British Museum

Central line tube from Oxford Circus going east calls at Tottenham Court Road, the nearest tube station to the museum, or you can walk along Oxford Street. Instead of looking at the high street stores (and keeping tabs on your money in case of pickpockets), think of the street when it was Tyburn Road, the one-way street to Tyburn tree – the gibbet where Marble Arch now stands – from Newgate Gaol. For centuries villains were dragged along here on hurdles or taken in carts through the crowds to be hanged in public. One wit stopped on the way to his execution to buy a bottle of wine. Instead of paying he called out to the innkeeper that he would pay him on the way back.

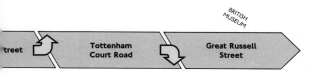

ILLUMINATING MANUSCRIPTS

The British Museum is found by turning up Tottenham Court Road and then turning right into Great Russell Street. It is free. My first port of call at the museum – after picking up a free plan from the information display opposite the main door – is always the cafeteria, a good place to plan what to see over a cup of coffee. Until 1993 the museum is the home of the British Library with its many treasures of world literature: Bede's eighth-century manuscript of the *History of the English Church and People*; the Anglo-Saxon poem *Beowulf* which is known only from the manuscript in the British Library; Magna Carta; handwritten notes by Walter Ralegh (note the spelling) for his *History of the World*, and so on – all displayed in the library galleries to the right of the main entrance.

TREASURES OF THE ANCIENT WORLD

It is not really a 'British' museum. It was founded in 1753 to house the extensive international collection of Sir Hans Sloane, physician and naturalist. His natural history collection went to form the nucleus of the Natural History Museum. The world-famous Elgin Marbles are here, removed from the frieze of the Parthenon at Athens at great expense (Greece would like them back), and the Rosetta Stone, which gave the clue about reading Egyptian hieroglyphs. Here too are fragile Egyptian mummies and the treasure from Sutton Hoo, the Anglo-Saxon ship burial.

BLOOMSBURY

Leave the British Museum by the north entrance. Facing you are the library and senate of the University of London. Further north, up Malet Street, is Dillon's bookshop and University College. Behind the college is Gordon Square,

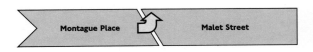

Montague Place   Malet Street

associated with the Bloomsbury Group. Before her marriage, Virginia Woolf lived at 46, a house later occupied by economist John Maynard Keynes. The critic and biographer Lytton Strachey lived at 51. Russell Square tube station, for Covent Garden and Walk 2, is on the north-east corner of Russell Square. If you prefer to walk the short distance, take the south exit from the British Museum, cut south through Museum Street and Drury Lane, and turn to the next walk when you reach Shorts Gardens.

If you are travelling to London around Christmas and the New Year, please note that most major attractions are closed. A few places are closed on Mondays. Most places in the City are closed on Saturdays and Sundays.

D Attractions with this logo make an effort to welcome the disabled. Other places are accessible with help. Phone for details. See also Disabled in London section. Popular attractions have a queuing system for telephone callers. You lose your place in the queue by re-dialling, so stay on the line.

St Edward's Tower, Westminster Cathedral, Victoria Street, SW1

071-834 7452
Adults 70p, Children & Concessions 30p
April to October daily 9.30-5
U St James's Park
Buses (to Victoria station) 2, 2A, 2B, 11, 16, 24, 25, 29, 36, 36A, 36B, 38, 39, 52, 52A, 73, 76, 82, 135, 177Ex, 185, 507, 510, C1
D Separate entrance to lift

Westminster Abbey, SW1

071-222 5152, Super Tours 071-222 7110
Super Tour (all of the below) £6.00 at regular intervals
Nave: Free. Mon-Sat 8-6 plus later opening Wed to 7.45, Sun between services except for worshippers
Royal Chapels, Poets' Corner: Adults £3.00, Under 16 60p, Concessions £1.50, With sound guide £4.00
Pyx Chamber, Chapter House, Undercroft Museum: Adults £1.60, Under 16 40p, Concessions 80p
Mon-Fri 9-4.45 (last admissions at 4), Saturdays 9-2.45 (last admissions at 2) and 3.45-5.45 (last admissions at 5)
Wednesdays 6-7.45 free entrance to all abbey
U Westminster
Buses 3, 11, 12, 24, 29, 53, 53X, 77, 77A, 88, 109, 159, 170, 177Ex, 184, 196, C1
D

Houses of Parliament, SW1

071-219 3000
Free. Open when Houses are in session
Visitors' Gallery House of Commons: Mon-Thur 2.30-10
or later, Fri 9.30-3
Visitors' Gallery House of Lords: Mon-Thur 3 to end of
debating, Fri 11 to end of debating (in afternoon)
Long queues, no baggage
U Westminster
Buses as to Westminster Abbey
D Phone
Other areas via your MP

Cabinet War Rooms, Clive Steps, King Charles Street, SW1

071-930 6961/071-416 5000
Adults £3.60, 5-16 £1.80, Concessions £2.70, Families
(2+2 or more) are offered free admission for one child
Taped guides in English, French, German, Italian, Spanish
and Japanese
Daily 10-6 (last admissions 5.15)
U Westminster
Buses 3, 11, 12, 24, 29, 53, 53X, 77, 77A, 88, 109, 159,
170, 177Ex, 184, 196
D

Banqueting House, Whitehall, SW1

071-930 4179
Adults £2.00, Children £1.35, Concessions £1.50
Mon-Sat 10-5 (last admissions 4.30)
U Westminster, Charing Cross
Buses as to Cabinet War Rooms
BR Charing Cross

Design Centre, 28 Haymarket, SW1

Free. Mon-Sat 10-6, Sun & Bank Holidays 1-6
U Piccadilly Circus
Buses 3, 6, 9, 12, 13, 14, 15, 15B, X15, 19, 22, 22B, 38,
53, 53X, 88, 159
D

Trocadero, Piccadilly Circus, W1
071-439 7331
Guinness World of Records: Adults £4.50, 4-15 £2.80,
Concessions £3.60
071-753 0800
Beatles Exhibition: Adults £4.00, 4-15 £2.50, Concessions
£3.50
Daily 10-10
U Piccadilly Circus
Buses as Design Centre
D

Rock Circus, London Pavilion, W1
071-734 7203, Recorded information 071-734 8025
Adults £5.75, Children £3.85, Concessions £4.85,
Families (2+2) £15.35
Mon, Wed, Thur, Sun 11-9, Tue 12-9, Fri & Sat 11-10
U Piccadilly Circus
Buses as Design Centre
D

Museum of Mankind, 6 Burlington Gardens, W1
071-437 2224
Free. Mon-Sat 10-5, Sun 2.30-6
U Green Park, Piccadilly Circus
Buses 9, 14, 19, 22, 25, 38
D Phone

British Museum, Great Russell Street, WC1
071-636 1555, Recorded information 071-580 1788
Free. Mon-Sat 10-5, Sun 2.30-6
U Tottenham Court Road, Russell Square, Holborn
Buses (to Tottenham Court Road) 7, 8, 10, 14, 14A, 19,
22B, 24, 25, 29, 38, 55, 73, 134, 176, 503
D Phone

Royal National Theatre

~~Gallery~~

~~River Terraces~~

~~Bookshop~~

Backstage Tours

~~Restaurant~~

~~Live Music~~

~~Cafe~~

Some theatre.

The Royal National Theatre is like no other - there's so much to choose from. Some things are free like our foyer concerts and exhibitions, or come and browse in our theatre Bookshop. And of course, the stunning views of London from our river terraces are free too!

We have three theatres offering a great choice, from dazzling comedy to classic tragedies. There are discounts for under 18's and students; or check on our low price weekday matinees and standby tickets. Each day we hold back some tickets for sale from 10am, so there's a chance of catching even our most popular productions, if you come early.

We have a restaurant, cafés and bars serving realistically priced refreshments at all times of the day. So spend some time at the National-without spending a fortune. Phone: 071-633 0880 for more information.

ROYAL NATIONAL THEATRE,
SOUTH BANK, LONDON SE1 9PX
FOYERS OPEN 10AM - 11PM
MONDAY - SATURDAY.

ROYAL
NATIONAL
THEATRE

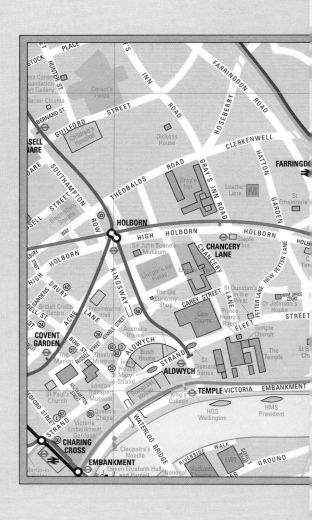

WALK 2

**COVENT GARDEN
ROYAL OPERA HOUSE
LINCOLN'S INN
FLEET STREET
OLD BAILEY
ST PAUL'S
BANK OF ENGLAND**

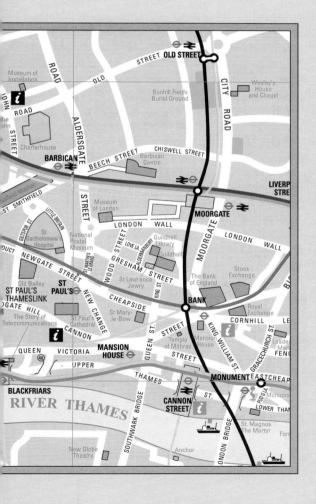

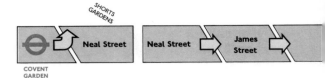

(Try not to do this walk on a Saturday as the Temple, Inns of Court and much of the City are closed.)

The whole day can be spent just at **Covent Garden**, browsing around the shops in the nearby streets and the stalls in the market. On emerging from the tube station on the corner of James Street, don't turn right straight away for the piazza. Turn left up Neal Street and stroll up as far as Shorts Gardens. Neal's Yard, just off this street, is a place for free-thinkers to buy anything from geranium oil to a crystal ball, and there is plenty to see even if you don't want to spend much money. The water clock above the wholefood warehouse is by Tim Hunkin, a modest genius with an eye for a working contraption who unites the concepts of art and science.

Returning down Neal Street to the piazza, you pass a hat shop which sells nothing but hats and is so small that customers have to queue in the street for entrance and a sheep shop which sells everything sheepish except dead meat. On the corner of the piazza is the Rock Garden restaurant, a cafe and rock venue which comes to life after dark.

Covent Garden

THE OTHER ST PAUL'S

Walk past the restaurant along King Street to the other end of the piazza to **St Paul's church**. The entrance is via an alleyway beyond the cnurch in King Street. The alley opens into a small and secluded garden, lit by ancient gas lamps, with benches for a packed lunch. Inside the

St Paul's church

church are memorials to English actors and actresses who live on in affectionate memory, such as Margaret Rutherford, Kenneth More and many others.

Retracing your steps back to the piazza, you can now see from the square that the elegant portico of St Paul's backs doorless onto the altar and is just for show. The church was designed by Inigo Jones in 1633 as part of his piazza built for the quality to promenade in. The portico, now a backdrop for street entertainers, was used by Shaw as the setting for the opening scene of 'Pygmalion' – which became the musical 'My Fair Lady'.

Here too was the first showing of a Punch and Judy show, and Punch and Judy can still be seen here from time to time. The toilets for Covent Garden are at this end but are inadequate for the crowds.

LONDON TRANSPORT MUSEUM

By Shaw's time the vegetable and fruit market had moved in and the central hall had been built. Overcrowding sent the early risers out of the centre of town to Nine Elms in 1974 and the piazza has gradually been reclaimed by the people. In the far corner lies the Old Flower Market, a glasshouse which is now the home of the **London Transport Museum**. There is a charge for the museum

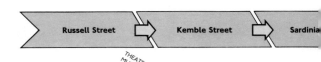

Russell Street · *THEATRE MUSEUM* · Kemble Street · Sardinia

but the entrance box is on the other side of the museum shop, and a free peep is possible. Both children and adults love to try the controls of a bus and a tube train. The spirit of each transport era has been captured by leading artists for London Transport's posters and this history of poster art is shown in the museum.

London Transport Museum

If you want to see it but are on a tight budget, you will find reproductions and postcards in the shop.

Passing through Russell Street, on your right is the coffee shop where Boswell met Dr Johnson in 1762 when it was Mr Davies's bookshop, and also the **Theatre**

Royal Opera House

Museum. Facing you at the end of the street is the **Theatre Royal**, Drury Lane. David Garrick and Dr Johnson came down to London together from Lichfield in 1737 to make their fortunes – which they did in their separate ways – and are now remembered together in Poets' Corner in Westminster Abbey.

BOW STREET

Drury Lane theatre and its near neighbour, now the **Royal Opera House**, in Bow Street, gave the old Bow Street police a difficult time in the years before they were disbanded in 1839. The magistrates employed six runners,

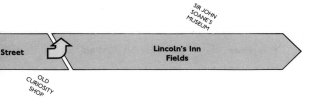

or plain-clothed thief-takers, from 1753, an idea of Henry Fielding, the novelist, who was chief Bow Street magistrate at the time. At least one runner used to be stationed in the foyer of the theatres to apprehend pickpockets. The old magistrates' office was opposite where the Victorian police court is now, approximately where the cars are parked behind the wire netting.

LINCOLN'S INN FIELDS

Continue across Bow Street and keep down Russell Street and Kemble Street until you reach Kingsway. All it has of interest is the old tram tunnel to Waterloo Bridge, underpassing the Aldwych. Cross over to Sardinia Street and you will see the **Old Curiosity Shop** in Portsmouth Street. This tiny shop sells old curiosities now, though there is some evidence that it was a heraldic sign-painter's shop in Dickens' day.

Turn around and walk northwards to the centre of the top edge of the fields (really a London square) to **Sir John Soane's Museum**, which is free. Sir John designed the Bank of England and left his house pretty much as it was when he was alive, a mini-British Museum of curios from all over the world in a domestic setting. It houses his architectural plans as well as Wren's grand plans for the post-Fire

Sir John Soane's Museum

London, which were never fully implemented. These can be seen by special appointment. Walking round the fields you pass the Old Hall, built in 1492 and the setting of

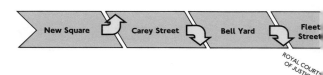

New Square ⟩ Carey Street ⟩ Bell Yard ⟩ Fleet Street

ROYAL COURTS OF JUSTICE

St Clement Danes

Dickens' 'Jarndyce v. Jarndyce' in *Bleak House*. Walk through New Square and turn left at Carey Street and right at Bell Yard to emerge in Fleet Street by the **Royal Courts of Justice**, built in the 1880s and described by John Mortimer as a 'misalliance between a French chateau and a Gothic cathedral'. Even its ancient urinals, he says, 'have a distinctly ecclesiastical appearance'. He doesn't mean the urinals under the street here, ancient though they are.

At the back of **St Clement Danes** church, which shares the traffic island with the inconveniences, is a statue of Samuel Johnson, Fleet Street's most famous inhabitant. He was a hack writer until he was asked to compile the dictionary that made him famous.

TEMPLE

Near where the dragon guards the entrance to the City at **Temple Bar** was once the printing house of Wynken de Worde. He was Caxton's apprentice who brought printing from movable type to the street in about 1500. At the bottom of Chancery Lane stands **Prince Henry's Room**, above a gateway leading to the Temple. The Great Fire of

ST CLEMENT DANES

ST DUNSTAN-IN-THE-WEST

Fleet Street

PRINCE HENRY'S ROOM

OLD COCK TAVERN

London came no further west than here, stopping just short of the building, which also miraculously survived the Blitz in 1940-41. It has been a tavern and Mrs Salmon's waxworks museum. Her effigies were eventually robbed for their clothes and accessories and vandalised in the last century, leaving a gap in the market for Madame Tussaud to fill so successfully.

The **Temple** takes its name from the Knights Templars of Jerusalem who established themselves as a wealthy monastic order in the twelfth century. The much restored round Temple church was modelled on the church of the Holy Sepulchre in Jerusalem and consecrated in 1185. The order was dissolved in 1312 by the Pope and the lands were given to the Knights Hospitallers, who leased much of it to the lawyers.

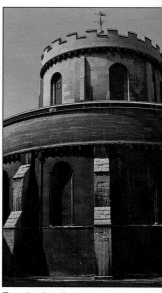

FLEET STREET

Back in Fleet Street again, *Temple church* the **Old Cock Tavern** close by the Temple boasts Johnson as a former client, but this was in a tavern of the same name a little further down the street. I planned to have lunch here while I wrote up this walk, but when I arrived I found it had been devastated in a fire and was full of dust and wheelbarrows. With any luck it will be just as good when it re-opens. Across the road near **St Dunstan-in-the-West** was where Sweeney Todd practised his murderous barbershop trade to provide

DR JOHNSON'S HOUSE   CHESHIRE CHEESE

Fleet Street

ST BRIDE'S CHURCH

fillings for Mrs Lovett's meat pies. He started out as a Victorian story published in Fleet Street called 'The String of Pearls' and soon passed into melodrama and folklore.

Much further down the street on the left is Bolt Court which leads to **Dr Johnson's House**, and the garret where the dictionary was compiled. The curators are welcoming and knowledgeable and the charge is not so great. Another tiny alley, Wine Office Court, leads to the **Cheshire Cheese**,

St Dunstan-in-the-West

re-built in 1667 yet with cellars that were once part of the much older Whitefriars monastery across the road. This busy restaurant serves traditional English fare in the upstairs dining room and is still owned by an independent brewery. Although there is a tiny bar on the ground floor dripping with atmosphere and old oak beams, there is barely room to turn round and it doesn't seem fair to clog up the narrow entrance just for a free look during peak eating hours. The building is undergoing some structural work in 1991 and may be closed.

Almost opposite (follow the brown signpost) is **St Bride's church**. The spire – impossible to see because of the buildings jammed up against the church – is said to have inspired a local baker to design the traditional tiered wedding cake. This is the printers' church and has a

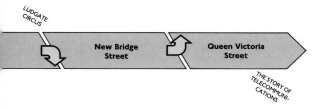

New Bridge Street

Queen Victoria Street

THE STORY OF TELECOMMUNI-CATIONS

history going back to Roman times – unusually so, because we are outside the old Roman city here. Creep into the crypt for a comprehensive history of the church and the street.

IN THE ARMS OF THE LAW

Coming back to Fleet Street, turn right for Ludgate Circus, once one of the entrances to the old walled city. Farringdon Road, running down to Blackfriars Bridge, is roughly the route of the Fleet River; at its southern end it is called New Bridge Street. Beneath your feet now are wharves, still with their mooring rings in place. Beside the river, too, once rose the Fleet debtors' prison.

FROM WIRES TO OPTICAL FIBRES

At Ludgate Circus, you can make a diversion from today's trail by turning right along New Bridge Street and then left into Queen Victoria Street. Walk about 100 yards and,

next to the Mermaid theatre, you will find **The Story of Telecommunications**. Here you can gain an insight into the influence of telecommunications on everyday life, from the early days to the present. Displays cover early telegraph apparatus together with the latest satellite and optical fibre technology. This is a hands-on museum in which you can fax messages, look down manholes and watch a ticker-tape machine in action.

St Bride's, Fleet Street

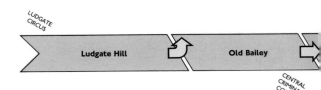

LUDGATE CIRCUS

Ludgate Hill   **Old Bailey**

CENTRAL CRIMINAL COURTS

It is irresistible to all ages. Return to Ludgate Circus to get back on today's route.

Climbing Ludgate Hill, with St Paul's in the background, turn left into Old Bailey, where you will find the **Central Criminal Courts**. If you want to see the old courts, where Crippen was tried in 1910, walk up to the top corner and queue in Newgate Street. Court proceedings in life are dreadfully slow going as the court reporters have to write everything down. Barristers shuffle their papers and 'hem' and 'haw' and 'hrrumph' and there is no button to press to fast forward to the verdict. The courts were built on the site of the old Newgate Gaol where public executions took place from 1783 to 1868.

BART'S

North of Old Bailey, via Giltspur Street, is **St Bartholomew's Hospital** – Bart's – founded in 1123 by the monk Rahere. As you approach Smithfield Meat Market at the top of Giltspur Street you should see to your right the half-timbered gatehouse which leads to the priory church of **St Bartholomew the Great**, founded at the same time. Rahere's tomb is here. This tranquil church survived the Fire of London and the Luftwaffe, though it fell into disuse for over 200 years and was used as a stable, a forge and a factory. Benjamin Franklin worked here in a printer's shop in 1724. There are some inexpensive workingmen's cafes around Smithfield.

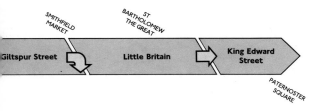

SMITHFIELD MARKET

ST BARTHOLOMEW THE GREAT

| Giltspur Street | Little Britain | King Edward Street |

PATERNOSTER SQUARE

ST PAUL'S

St Paul's is approached by turning left directly out of the church gateway and the dome can soon be seen. Outside the **National Postal Museum** is a statue to Rowland Hill, who invented not just the penny post but with it the adhesive postage label, or 'stamp' as it was soon to be called. Paternoster Square is reached by going up some steps and through an appallingly boring office block into a desolate square with only a statue of the Shepherd and His flock to enrich the experience. It's almost unbelievable

St Paul's Cathedral

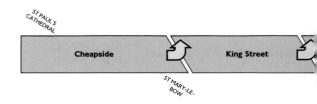

that such a bleak place can exist side by side with Wren's masterpiece.

The cathedral is free for a few yards but if you wish to see anything interesting adults, at least, have to pay. Most of the nation's notables are buried in Westminster Abbey, but here are Nelson and Wellington, who met only once in life. Wren himself, who lived to be 91, is buried here. If you want to go up high you can go even further up than the two galleries in the dome. A doorway leads to a sinister black space between the outer dome of the roof and the inner dome of the ceiling. A staircase hanging in this space leads up to a stone balcony where you can briefly view London and the river before being forced down the other staircase by the flow of foot traffic. You need to be fit. The cathedral is honeycombed with passages and doorways which were all known like the backs of their hands by the wartime firewatchers of St Paul's who risked their lives night after night during the Blitz.

CHEAPSIDE

Come out of St Paul's and make your way around the cathedral to find Cheapside, once the City's main shopping street, and the church of **St Mary-le-Bow**. The mark of a true cockney is to be born within the sound of Bow bells. A bell in this church used to ring in the fifteenth century at 9 o'clock in the evening to tell the apprentices to stop work, and it was this bell, heard at Highgate, that made Dick Whittington turn back. If the bells can be heard as far away as Highgate then just about *everyone* born in London is a cockney.

Whittington was not a legendary figure, but a real man, Mayor and public benefactor, who founded the **Guildhall Library**, and in whose lifetime the **Guildhall** building was started. These two are to be found off Cheapside by going up Aldermanbury. The library, now in

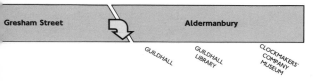

Gresham Street   Aldermanbury

GUILDHALL   GUILDHALL LIBRARY   CLOCKMAKERS' COMPANY MUSEUM

St Mary-le-Bow

a modern building, is open to the public. It has an interesting little bookshop and sometimes has exhibitions near the foyer. The **Clockmakers' Company Museum** is here, which it is best to visit at 11 or 12 for the chimes.

Guildhall's Great Hall is also open to the public. It lost

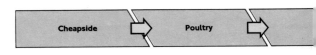

Cheapside ⇨ Poultry ⇨

its roof in the Great Fire and again in the Blitz, when it also lost the figures of Gog and Magog, the legendary giants. These have been replaced and stand at the far end of the Great Hall. There was a function at Guildhall on the day I tried to visit. This is one of the hazards of trying to see the place. Write in advance for a tour of the Great Hall, Old Library and Crypt.

BANK

Cheapside gives way to Poultry which, like Bread Street and Milk Street, recalls the mediaeval trades and shops in the area. At the end of the street is the **Bank of England** – the Old Lady of Threadneedle Street – which now has a free museum within its walls. The museum re-creates the old stock office, designed by Sir John Soane in 1793, and takes the visitor through the history of the banknote and its forgeries as well as through the history of the bank itself. They keep some real gold at the museum so security

The Royal Exchange

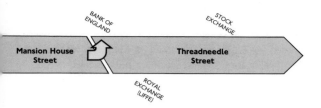

guards are necessary. Don't let this put you off as they are very friendly and the museum is unique.

The **Stock Exchange** is almost next door but not open to visitors since the bomb in 1990. To see the City at work try LIFFE, London International Financial Futures Exchange at the **Royal Exchange**. Here at lunchtimes the trading can be watched from the visitors' gallery while video displays explain how the market works. The **Mansion House**, on the other corner of this busy crossroads, is not open to the public unless you have committed a misdemeanour in the City as, apart from being the home of the Lord Mayor of London, the Mansion House is the City's magistrates' court where the aldermen sit in justice. It is from here on the second Saturday in November that the annual Lord Mayor's Show sets forth with bands, floats and new Lord Mayor in a golden coach.

If you want to connect up with Walk 3, which starts at the Monument, just walk down King William Street. If you want a break first, now would be a good time to detour to Leadenhall Market for a snack (see Markets section) via Cornhill.

If you are travelling to London around Christmas and the New Year, please note that most major attractions are closed. A few places are closed on Mondays. Most places in the City are closed on Saturdays and Sundays.

D Attractions with this logo make an effort to welcome the disabled. Other places are accessible with help. Phone for details. See also Disabled in London section. Popular attractions have a queuing system for telephone callers. You lose your place in the queue by re-dialling, so stay on the line.

London Transport Museum, Covent Garden, WC2
071-379 6344, Recorded information 071-836 8557
Adults £3.00, 5-16 and Concessions £1.50, Families (2+2) £7.00
Daily 10-6 (last admissions 5.15)
U Covent Garden
Buses (along the Strand) 1, 6, 9, 11, 13, 15, 15B, X15, 77, 77A, 170, 176, 177Ex, 196; (down Charing Cross Road) 24, 29, 176
D Free

Theatre Museum, Russell Street, WC2
071-836 7891
Adults £2.50, Children & Concessions £1.50
Tue-Sun 11-7 (last admissions 6.30)
U Covent Garden
Buses as for London Transport Museum
D

Sir John Soane's Museum, 13 Lincoln's Inn Fields, WC2
071-405 2107
Free. Tue-Sat 10-5
U Holborn
Buses 8, 17, 18, 22B, 25, 45, 46, 171A, 243, 259, 501 to Chancery Lane
D Phone

Prince Henry's Room, 17 Fleet Street, EC4
071-353 7323

Free. Mon-Fri 1.45-5, Sat 1.45-4.30
Buses 4, 6, 9, 11, 15, 15B, X15, 171A, 502, 513

Dr Johnson's House, 17 Gough Square, Fleet Street, EC4
071-353 3745
Adults £1.50, Concessions £1.00
May to September Mon-Sat 11-5.30; October to April
Mon-Sat 11-5
U Temple, Blackfriars
Buses as to Prince Henry's Room

Telecom Technology Showcase, 135 Queen Victoria Street, EC4
Recorded information 0800 289689
Free. Mon-Fri 10-6; closed Bank Holidays
U Blackfriars, St Paul's
Buses (to Blackfriars Bridge) 45, 59, 63, 76, 141, 184
D Phone

Central Criminal Court, Newgate Street and Old Bailey, EC4
071-248 3277
U St Paul's

National Postal Museum, King Edward Street, EC1
071-239 5420
Free. Mon-Thur 9.30-4.30, Fri 9.30-4
U St Paul's
Buses as to St Paul's or Museum of London
D Phone

St Paul's Cathedral, EC4
071-248 2705
Donation Adults £1.00, Under 16 60p
Galleries Adults £2.70, Under 16 & Senior citizens £1.10, Students £1.85
Crypt Adults £1.70, Under 16 70p, Students £1.15
Ambulatory Adults £1.00, Students 50p, Under 16 & Senior citizens free
Galleries, crypt and ambulatory: Mon-Fri 10-4.15, Sat 11-4.15

Sung Evensong 5 pm daily (not August when choir on tour). The crypt may be closed for services.
Guided tours Adults £5.00, Under 16 & Senior citizens £2.50, Students £4.00
Mon-Sat unless service 11 am, 11.30, 2 pm, 2.30
U St Paul's
Buses 4, 8, 22B, 25, 141, 501, 502
D Access to main body and crypt with helper

City Information Centre in St Paul's Churchyard
071-606 3030

Guildhall, off Gresham Street, EC2P 2EJ
Free to Great Hall daily 10-5 provided there is no functic on. Free tour by written application to The Keeper includes Old Library and Crypt.
U Bank
Buses as to St Paul's and walk along Cheapside
D Limited but improving, phone

Clockmakers' Company Collection, Guildhall Library, EC2
071-606 3030
Free. Mon-Fri 9.30-5
U Bank
Buses as to St Paul's and walk along Cheapside
D Phone

Bank of England Museum, EC2
071-601 5793
Free. Mon-Fri 10-5
U Bank
Buses 6, 8, 9, 11, 15B, X15, 21, 22B, 25, 43, 76, 133, 149, 214, 501 to Bank
D Phone

Stock Exchange, Old Broad Street, EC2
071-588 2355, ext 29770
Closed. Phone for latest information.
U Bank
Buses as for Bank Museum
D Phone

LIFFE, Royal Exchange, EC3
071-623 0444
Free. Mon-Fri 11.30-1.45
U Bank
Buses as for Bank Museum

Mansion House, EC4N 8BH
Free. Tue-Thur 11-2 by written application to the Principal
Assistant
U Bank
Buses as for Bank Museum

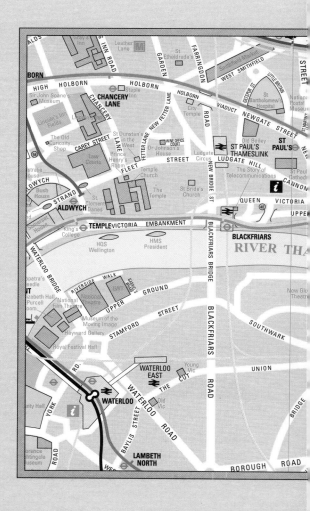

MONUMENT
TOWER
ST KATHARINE'S DOCK
TOWER BRIDGE
SOUTHWARK
SOUTH BANK

WALK 3

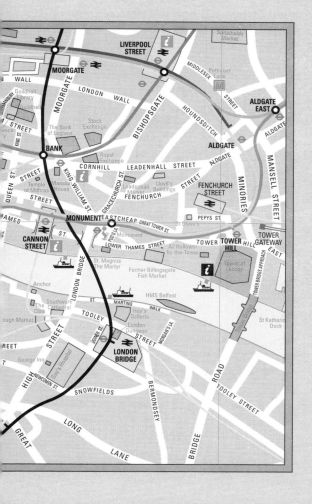

Fish Street Hill   Monument Street

MONUMENT   MONUMENT

Try not to visit the City of London on a Saturday. Much of it is closed, including places to eat, public conveniences and some churches. It is on Saturday that the heavy building work can be done and the traffic dies down to give way to enormous cranes and the sound of drills. A weekday is best, when people are about their money-making and the street scene is full of interest.

The City has always been the heart of London since the Romans picked this hillside by the Thames as their major city and constructed a wooden bridge from immense tree trunks at the foot of what is now Fish Street Hill. Coming out of Monument station ignore the twentieth-century crashing and banging about you and look downhill to the river. You should be looking down Fish Street Hill. Behind you Gracechurch Street continues the old Roman road towards the basilica and other administrative buildings, now under Leadenhall Market.

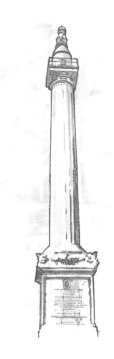

MONUMENT

The **Monument** itself, by Wren, is the monument to the Great Fire of London and for nearly three centuries visitors have climbed its 311 steps to recall the shocking day in 1666 when flames licked up from a baker's shop in Pudding

Monument

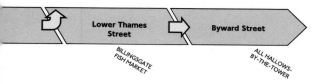

Lower Thames
Street

BILLINGSGATE
FISH MARKET

Byward Street

ALL HALLOWS-
BY-THE-TOWER

Lane, 202 feet away (the height of the Monument) to start a fire that demolished over 80 churches and 13,000 homes, yet only 6 people died. Thousands had died in the Great Plague the previous year.

Walk down Monument Street and see across Lower Thames Street the handsome sandy brick and stone building of the former **Billingsgate Fish Market**, for centuries the centre of Britain's fish trade. There had been a market here since Saxon times but the fishmongers moved to a bigger and better site in Docklands in 1982, leaving the elegant Victorian building to be redeveloped. Don't try to cross the dual carriageway here, but look across at the old market. To your right is the church of **St Magnus the Martyr**, one of the few relics of our Scandinavian invaders. Magnus was a prince of Norway in the eleventh century.

SAMUEL PEEPS ...

Walk along the north side of Lower Thames Street and follow the traffic as it bears left up the hill until you see the elaborate spire of **All Hallows-by-the-Tower**. Samuel Pepys stood on the tiny balcony of the spire to view the devastation caused by the Great Fire. Those on a budget might prefer the friendly atmosphere of this interesting church to the frenetic commercialism of the Tower. It has an Undercroft Museum,

All Hallows-by-the-Tower

> **Tower Hill**

associations with William Penn as well as Pepys, a brass rubbing centre, a restaurant and, of course, an appeal. All the London churches are desperately short of cash and the chink of coins in the box provided always makes a good impression.

... ACROSS TO THE TOWER ...

The **Tower** offers traditional London fare. Tom Vernon (of 'Fat Man on a Bicycle' fame) describes tradition as an event almost entirely surrounded by tourists. Here, decked out for tradition/tourists, are the Yeoman Warders of Henry VII. Unlike the guards at Westminster, the Beefeaters will talk to visitors and act as guides.

The Keep – the White Tower – was built by William the Conqueror in 1078 and made pretty by Wren. In the Bloody Tower were found the skeletons of two youngsters in the reign of Charles II. They were buried in Westminster Abbey as the uncrowned Edward V and his

The Tower

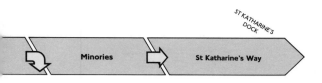

younger brother Richard – the princes in the Tower. Speculation about their murder has taxed historians ever since. I don't believe that Richard III ordered their death in 1483, as he had no motive. The princes were not imprisoned in the Tower, they lived there because for part of its history it was a royal palace. It has also been a zoo (until 1834), an observatory, a mint and a treasury. The Crown Jewels, the world's richest regalia,

The White Tower

are still here, though there is usually a queue. The royal armouries are at the Tower and some idea of the size of Henry VIII can be gained from his armour.

... TO SEE THE SHIPS ...

A signposted walkway leads round the Tower, passing, on your left across the road, Tower Hill tube station and one of the public execution sites of old London. Follow signposts to **St Katharine's Dock**, with its marina of tall

St Katharine's Dock

Tower Bridge → Tower Bridge Road →

ships and cruisers moored alongside curious shops and cafes. The Dickens pub needs no advertising here, and is now set in an apartment complex designed in Instant Picturesque, a horizontal pastiche style on a human scale and not noticeably over-influenced by profit.

... GO UNDER THE BRIDGE

Wind your way back to **Tower Bridge** and either go

Tower Bridge

under the bridge where you will find a caff (for overseas visitors: this is not quite the same as a 'cafe', but is the English term for an un-pretentious kind of tea-room which may be without toilet facilities) or/and then re-trace your steps to the downstream side of the

bridge to find the steps up. You don't have to pay to walk across the bridge. The entrance fee is for the museum in the towers and the walkway which connects them. You can also see the bridge machinery at the south side – but you have to buy the ticket on the bridge. It always seems surprising that such a feature of London was built only in 1894. When Pepys looked out from the spire of All Hallows he may have seen ships and the Tower, but he saw no bridge here.

If you didn't climb the Monument you should really go up here for a helicopter's eye view of London – the new Docklands rising from years of neglect to the east, the City perched on its hilltop, and Westminster, with the Houses of Parliament snuggling round the river's bend. If you are lucky the bridge will open, but this happens only a couple of times a week, if that.

HMS BELFAST

HAY'S GALLERIA

BATTLESHIP GREY

The grey battleship upstream of the Tower is *HMS Belfast*, the last survivor of the Royal Navy's big gun ships. She saw service in the Second World War and Korea and was saved from the scrapyard in the 1960s to become a floating museum. When construction work is finished

HMS Belfast

nearby it should be possible to reach *HMS Belfast* along the embankment from the Tower, but at the time of writing (September 1990) hoardings bar the route and a detour has to be made along Tooley Street almost as far as Hay's Wharf before finding a way through to the ship.

Tooley Street makes no effort to cheer the visitor. It is representative of much of London away from the tourist trail, especially on the south side of the river and in the East End; and for this it is worth looking at. Why is it so important for a business to have an address in the City across the water when Tooley Street is only a mile away?

Hay's Galleria

SANTA'S GROTTO

At **Hay's Galleria**, once a Victorian warren of wharves and warehouses, it is Christmas all the year round, as the Christmas decoration shop testifies. Prestigious offices, cafes and high street stores are in graceful, calm surroundings

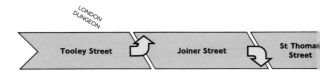

The George, Southwark

here, cool in the heat, dry in the winter. 'The Navigators' provides a focal point. This intriguing and delightful fantasy sculpture captures the spirit of England's nautical and pioneering history. Pause for a cappuccino in the corner cafe before returning to Tooley Street.

Across the road is the **London Dungeon**. I have to admit I gave it a miss, though queues along the street testify to its ghoulish popularity.

GUY'S AND ST THOMAS'

Turn left here underneath London Bridge station down Joiner Street, a spooky Dickensian tunnel that comes out in St Thomas Street. Turn right into the street. On the left is Guy's Hospital (the modern hospital buildings rise behind the courtyard you can see here). On the right used to stand St Thomas' Hospital, which moved to Lambeth over 100 years ago. All that remains is the **Old Operating Theatre and Herb Garret** above the church. Keats was a pupil in 1817 at the medical school which served Guy's and St Thomas' and Florence Nightingale founded her school of nursing at St Thomas' later in the century.

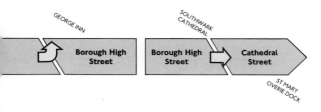

SOUTHWARK

Press on to the corner and turn left down Borough High Street. A little further down the street, down George Alley, is the **George**, the last galleried inn in London. The present building dates from 1676 though an earlier version existed in Shakespeare's time and possibly before

that. It was from the Tabard Inn a few yards away (once in Talbot Yard) that Chaucer's pilgrims set out on their journey to Canterbury, and Sam Weller met Mr Pickwick for the first time at the White Hart (formerly in White Hart Yard). The main road here leads to London Bridge, and the presence of so many inns is because the bridge – until 1750 the only bridge across the Thames – was a toll bridge and shut at night to leave travellers stranded.

Now walk back towards the bridge, but instead of crossing, go down the steps to **Southwark Cathedral**, a place of worship since

Southwark Cathedral

Saxon times but a cathedral only since 1905. John Harvard, founder of the American university, was baptised here in 1607, the same year that Shakespeare's brother Edmund, who is buried here, died of the plague.

Outside, turn right to St Mary Overie Dock and the schooner *Kathleen and May*, run by the Maritime Trust. Cross the road and follow signs to the **Clink** prison in

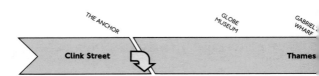

THE ANCHOR   GLOBE MUSEUM   GABRIEL'S WHARF

Clink Street   **Thames**

Clink Street. Once upon a time this prison, which gave its name to all others, was the private prison of the bishops of Winchester. It is advertised as being 'on the site' of the old prison.

The **Anchor**, at the end of Clink Street, is one of the dozens of taverns which made this a sort of Tudor and Stuart Soho. The seventeenth-century building was destroyed by fire and this building, with its fine beams, dates from the eighteenth century. Dr Johnson is said to have been a regular here – a claim made by all eighteenth-century London taverns?

GLOBAL WARNING

Walk along the river from here and follow the signs to the **Globe Museum**. The original Globe theatre was sited half under the approach to Southwark road bridge so is being reconstructed on Bankside in an impressive bid to bring Shakespeare's theatre to life. The museum is inexpensive and worth a slight detour.

Of Bankside itself, all that remains of interest is the house at **49 Cardinal's Wharf** where Wren stayed while building St Paul's. The cathedral is disappearing from view

The National Theatre

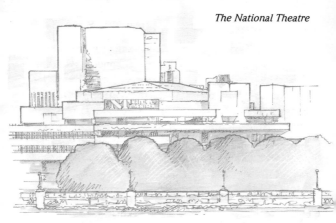

NATIONAL THEATRE QUEEN ELIZABETH HALL HAYWARD GALLERY NATIONAL FILM THEATRE ROYAL FESTIVAL HALL MOMI

Embankment

across the river. Continue along the river walk past the power station and arrive at the southern end of Blackfriars Bridge. Look carefully at the far bank beneath the pillars of the railway bridge. The seething in the water is caused by the arrival at the Thames of one of London's lost rivers, the Fleet, which runs down the length of Farringdon Road.

SOUTH BANK

Cross the approach road to **Blackfriars Bridge** and make your way down to the embankment again, keeping on the south side of the river. Here at low tide can still be seen the wood and cobbled slips for launching working Thames boats. Continue as far as **Gabriel's Wharf**. This array of shops is not quite what it seems. The row of houses facing you is in fact skilfully painted on a blank warehouse wall. The artists themselves are looking out of one of the painted windows at you. The area has a

The National Film Theatre

cafe, a Friday market and shops for London craftspeople.

Next door is the headquarters of London Weekend Television and the concrete culture complex of the **National Theatre, Hayward Gallery, Queen Elizabeth Hall, National Film Theatre, Royal Festival Hall** and **Museum of the Moving Image**. On Saturdays books and prints are sold in the shelter of Waterloo Bridge and there is a reasonably priced cafe at the Royal Festival Hall with a river view.

To connect with Walk 4, walk across Hungerford

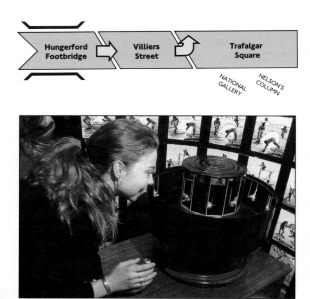

Museum of the Moving Image

Footbridge to Villiers Street and turn left at the top to find yourself in Trafalgar Square. The bridge shakes when a train for Charing Cross goes across but you are quite safe. If the walk is a little too far try getting a number 1 or 176 over Waterloo Bridge and down the Strand to Trafalgar Square, or a 184 from Stamford Street, which goes over Westminster Bridge, past Big Ben and down Whitehall.

If you are travelling to London around Christmas and the New Year, please note that most major attractions are closed. A few places are closed on Mondays. Most places in the City are closed on Saturdays and Sundays.

D Attractions with this logo make an effort to welcome the disabled. Other places are accessible with help. Phone for details. See also Disabled in London section. Popular attractions have a queuing system for telephone callers. You lose your place in the queue by re-dialling, so stay on the line.

Monument, Monument Street, EC2
071-626 2717
Adults £1.00, Under 16 25p
April to September Mon-Fri 9-6, weekends 2-6 (last admissions 5.40); October to March Mon-Sat 9-4 (last admissions 3.40)
U Monument, Bank
Buses 15, 21, 22A, 25, 35, 40, 43, 44, 47, 48, 133, 214, 501, 505, 510, 513, D1

Tower of London, Tower Hill, EC3
071-709 0765
Adults £5.90, 5-15 £3.70, Concessions £4.50
Free guided tours by the Yeoman Warders
March to October Mon-Sat 9.30-6.30 (last admissions at 5), Sun 2-6 (last admissions at 5); November to February Mon-Sat 9.30-4 (last admissions at 3); Crown Jewels closed January
U Tower Hill
DLR Tower Gateway
Buses 15, X15, 25, 42, 78, 100, 510, D1
D Phone, limited

Tower Bridge, SE1
071-407 0922
Adults £2.50, Children & Senior citizens £1.00
April to October daily 10-6.30 (last admissions at 5.45); November to March daily 10-4.45 (last admissions at 4)
U Tower Hill
DLR Tower Gateway

Buses 42, 78 and 510 cross the bridge itself, other buses as the Tower
D

HMS Belfast, Morgan's Lane, Tooley Street, SE1
071-407 6434/071-403 6246
Adults £3.50, 5-16 £1.75, Concessions £1.75, Families (2+2) £9.00
20 March to 31 October daily 10-5.20 (last admissions);
1 November to 19 March 10-4 (last admissions)
U BR London Bridge
Buses 42, 47, 78, 510, P11 (P11 runs parallel to the river as far as Waterloo station)

London Dungeon, 28-34 Tooley Street, SE1
071-403 0606
Adults £5.00, Students £4.00, Children & Senior citizens £3.00
October to Easter daily 10-4.30 (last admissions);
Easter to September 10-5.30 (last admissions)
U BR London Bridge
Buses as *HMS Belfast*
D Free entry if in wheelchair
Long queues

Operating Theatre, Museum and Herb Garret, 9a St Thomas Street, SE1
071-955 5000 (Guy's Hospital) ext 4791
Adults £1.00, Children & Concessions 60p
Mon, Wed, Fri 12.30-4
U BR London Bridge
Buses as *HMS Belfast*

Kathleen and May, St Mary Overie Dock, SE1
Adults £1.00, Children 50p
Mon-Fri 10-5, summer weekends only 11-4
U BR London Bridge
Buses P11, 17, 42, 44, 47, 78, 510

The Clink Exhibition, 1 Clink Street, SE1
071-403 6515/071-378 1558
Adults £2.00, Concessions £1.00, Family £5.00

Daily 10-6
U BR London Bridge
Buses as *Kathleen and May*

Globe Museum, Bear Gardens, Bankside, SE1
071-620 0202
Adults £2.00 Under 16 & Concessions £1.00
Mon-Sat 10-5.30, Sun 1.30-5
U BR London Bridge
Buses P11, 149

Gabriel's Wharf
Friday market 11-3; Shops, normal opening hours
U BR Waterloo
Buses P11, 149
D

London Weekend Television
Write to LWT, Ticket office, South Bank, SE1, for free
tickets to shows but expect a long wait.

National Theatre, South Bank, SE1
071-928 2252
U BR Waterloo
Buses (to Waterloo) P11, 1, 4, 68, 68X, 76, 149, 168,
171, 171A, 176, 188, 501, 502, 505, 507, 513, C1, D1

Hayward Gallery, South Bank, SE1
071-928 3144, Recorded information 071-261 0127
Adults £4.00 (£2.50 on Mon), Concessions £2.50
Tue & Wed 10-8, Thur-Mon 10-6
U BR Waterloo
Buses as for National Theatre
D

**South Bank Centre (Queen Elizabeth Hall, Royal
Festival Hall, Purcell Room), SE1**
Box office 071-928 8800, Information 071-928 3002,
Recorded information 071-633 0932
U BR Waterloo
Buses as for National Theatre
D

National Film Theatre, South Bank, SE1
071-928 3232
U BR Waterloo
Buses as for National Theatre
D

Museum of the Moving Image, South Bank, SE1
071-928 3535, Recorded information 071-401 2636
Adults £4.95, Students £4.20, Children & Senior citizens
£3.50, Family (2+4 max) £15.00
Tue-Sat 10-8, Sun, Bank Holidays and half-term Mondays
10-6 (last admissions one hour before closing)
U BR Waterloo
Buses as for National Theatre
D

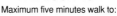

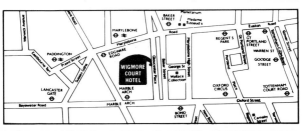

WALK 4

TRAFALGAR SQUARE
NATIONAL GALLERY
BUCKINGHAM PALACE
HARRODS
MUSEUMS
ROYAL ALBERT HALL
MARBLE ARCH

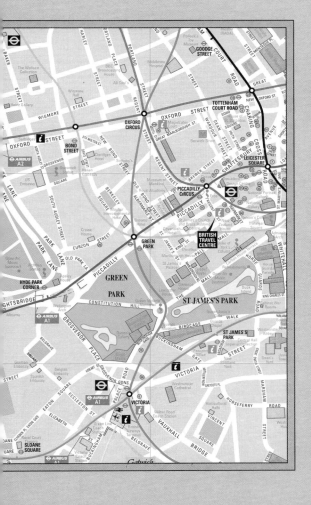

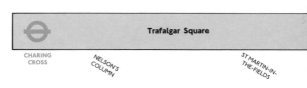

CHARING
CROSS

NELSON'S
COLUMN

Trafalgar Square

ST MARTIN-IN-
THE-FIELDS

Today's tour starts at Charing Cross tube station for **Trafalgar Square** and Nelson, the one-armed victor of Trafalgar, gazing in his one-eyed fashion down Whitehall from his podium, 51 metres of Devon granite, topped

Trafalgar Square

by a statue 6 metres high. Before it was erected, to celebrate Nelson's victory over Napoleon at the battle of Trafalgar, fourteen men sat down to dinner on the plinth. The square is the hub of street life in London, and has been almost since it was built in the 1840s, especially for political demonstrations and protest marchers. It is also popular at Christmas, when the raising of the giant Norway spruce marks the start of the season, and on New Year's Eve when crowds meet to sing 'Auld Lang Syne' by the fountains to the chimes of Big Ben. But don't drink the water from the fountains or you will turn into a pigeon, like so many before you.

The church of **St Martin-in-the-Fields**, in the north-east corner of the square, is the parish church of the Admiralty, and has a programme of concerts listed in the porch (£4 is the cheapest seat). Nell Gwyn is buried here. The crypt has a free art gallery, a brass rubbing centre, shop and cafeteria.

St Martin-in-the-Fields

National Portrait Gallery

UP TO DATE, DOWN TO EARTH

Moving north, pass the monument to Nurse Edith Cavell who died in the First World War forgiving her German executioners, and enter the **National Portrait Gallery** (free). Nelson is here too, on the top floor. The pictures get more recent as you descend towards the ground floor. Mrs Thatcher was at the top of the stairs leading to the basement toilets when I visited. They may have had to move her in a Major reshuffle.

The short-sighted might find the gallery frustrating as the names of the distinguished deceased are tiny and have to be scrutinised nose to nameplate, whereas the actual portraits are best admired from a distance. As you come forward in time towards the ground floor the men in the portraits start to appear all in black, the official uniform of the city gent even today. This was a fashion set in Regency London by Beau Brummell, who never wore anything else. Who would have thought that this individual vanity would have had such a phenomenal effect?

THE NATIONAL GALLERY

Back into the square, turn right for the main entrance to the **National Gallery** itself (free), which has over 2000 masterpieces. These include John Constable's *The Haywain* and one of

National Gallery

Trafalgar Square

KING CHARLES I STATUE

ADMIRALTY ARCH

Rembrandt's self-portraits. Those of us who witnessed the Beatles' rise to fame will remember the stolen Goya of the Duke of Wellington. Fortunately it was discovered on a rubbish tip and it hangs on the ground floor under the eagle eye of the security guard. The gallery also has Bronzino's *Allegory*. Monty Python fans will recognise the foot on the left of the picture as the one which inspired Terry Gilliam's animations. The lower ground floor restaurant has good coffee in pleasant surroundings. There may even be fresh flowers in the Ladies.

BIRD'S-EYE VIEW

Pause on the balcony over-looking Trafalgar Square and look around you. Straight ahead, south, is Whitehall and the corridors of power. The seated horseman well below Nelson is King Charles I, gazing down Whitehall to where he lost his head in 1649. He is on the site of the original Charing Cross, where the funeral procession of the *'chère reine'* of Edward I

King Charles I

rested on its way to Westminster Abbey in 1290. Look west (to your right) towards Pall Mall, the heart of clubland. Behind you, to the north, are theatreland and the bookshops of Charing Cross Road, and east is the Strand, an ancient road which once ran literally along the shore of the Thames before the embankment was built.

VISITING ROYALTY

Cross the square now to reach Admiralty Arch, built in 1910 as part of a national memorial to Queen Victoria.

The Mall

INSTITUTE OF CONTEMPORARY ARTS

The central arch is closed to all except the sovereign. The pink-surfaced **Mall** stretches nearly a mile to Buckingham Palace. On the right is the **Institute of Contemporary Arts**, underneath the elegant Nash Terrace·(small day-membership charge), scene of many controversial avant-garde exhibitions. It

The Mall

has a small theatre, a cinema and a reasonably priced restaurant, but does not open until 12. Along the Mall is **St James's Park** on the left with its lake, pelicans and

St James's Park

occasional flamingos. The daffodils are spectacular in the spring. Nearer the palace on the right is **Marlborough House**, originally built by the first Duke of Marlborough for his Duchess, Sarah. Further on is St James's Palace, built by Henry VIII and containing state apartments by Wren. The gatehouse has the initials of Henry and the ill-fated Anne Boleyn carved over the doors. The mansion was built over a med-

iaeval leper colony and was the royal residence in London from 1698 until the new Queen Victoria preferred to live in Buckingham Palace. Even today ambassadors are appointed to the Court of St James, a hangover from pre-Victorian times. The palace is not open to the public for

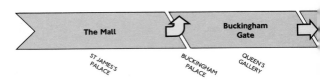

The Mall | Buckingham Gate

ST JAMES'S PALACE | BUCKINGHAM PALACE | QUEEN'S GALLERY

security reasons, though early risers on a winter Sunday may find the **Chapel Royal** open for worship. The Queen Mother lives in **Clarence House**, in this complex.

'CHRISTOPHER ROBIN WENT DOWN WITH ALICE'

Arrive at **Buckingham Palace** shortly after 11 for the 11.30 changing of the guard, which takes half an hour. See Traditional events section for details. Everyone should see the changing of the guard at least once. The red-coated guards in their bearskins are not just decorative. They carry useful grey machine-guns which make you realise with a sudden chill that times have changed since 'Christopher Robin went down with Alice' to see the ceremony. The palace is not impressively old. It was started in 1703 and was only completed in 1913 when the front was faced with Portland stone. If the Queen is at home the Royal Standard flies from the flagpole.

ROUND THE PALACE WALLS

Keep the palace walls on your right and follow them round as far as the **Queen's Gallery**, the only portion of

ROYAL MEWS | Buckingham Palace Road | Grosvenor Place | APSLEY HOUSE

the palace open to the public, which presents special exhibitions from the royal collection and is not too dear. A note on the booking desk regrets that there are no toilet facilities. Further along Buckingham Palace Road is the **Royal Mews**, open two afternoons a week (usually) to show the state coaches, again for quite a small charge. The royal cars are housed in another wing of the old stables and can sometimes be seen driving through the main yard.

If you walk round the corner from the mews you will be in Grosvenor Place. Follow the road, still keeping the palace gardens and wall on your right. Behind the wall is a naturally landscaped area with trees and a lake where the royal garden parties are held, but on this side of the wall there is little for the moment to attract the visitor. Press on up to Hyde Park Corner, a traffic nightmare, and enter the Hyde Park Corner subway, the only way to get across the road. If you have £2 to spare, visit **Apsley House**, on the corner of Park Lane, once the home of the Duke of Wellington, victor of Waterloo. He later became prime minister and one of the most eminent Victorians of them all.

Buckingham Palace

Knightsbridge

ROTTEN ROW

Apsley House

WELLINGTON AND WATERLOO

The security guard will search your bags for sandwiches, or so he says with a smile, and let you through. A larger-than-life-size sculpture of Napoleon in the style of a Greek god, naked except for a rather small fig-leaf, stands alone and palely loitering in the stairwell. Upstairs the Waterloo Gallery was once the setting for the annual Waterloo dinner. The day I went fresh orchids were being arranged in huge jardinières and vases, and an artist was at work quietly copying one of the paintings. The windows look out over Hyde Park and the nineteenth century.

BEAU MONDE

Back into the frantic screech of the late twentieth century, retreat into the subway again and come up this time on the south side of Knightsbridge to window-shop down towards Harrods. Across the road is the edge of Hyde Park, with the brown track of **Rotten Row** running parallel. This was the *Route du Roi* – the king's way – much frequented by Regency beaux and still the favourite

Brompton Road

BROMPTON ORATORY

of London's horse-riders. Its tercentenary was celebrated in 1990.

A little further on, near Albert Gate, is the spot where two mediaeval knights fought to the death on the bridge over the River Westbourne, which still flows underneath the streets to its outlet in the Thames – hence the name 'Knightsbridge'.

HARRODS

Bear left after Knightsbridge tube station to go down Brompton Road, and the familiar outline of **Harrods** soon presents itself. Not everything is costly in Harrods, and the well-trained staff are always polite. The best plan is to take the lift or escalators to the top floor and spiral down to the ground floor and the amazing food halls. You can buy anything from a T-shirt to a palatial bath that would take the servants all day to fill with pitchers from the basement of the ancestral hall. Or if the fancy takes you, why not browse round the book department while the embroidery service

Harrods

monograms your satin bedlinen? Authors often have book signings at Harrods, which adds interest to the day. There are various coffee lounges dotted about the store, and the fourth floor Ladies, near the Georgian restaurant, is recommended for a final stop for the beauty of its sanitary fittings – gentlemen will have to admire the decor of the Gents for themselves. Continue down Brompton Road for **Brompton Oratory**, a late Victorian Catholic church,

Thurloe Place   **Exhibition Road**

V & A

white and gleaming on the outside, candlelit and muted tones on the inside. It is almost next to the **Victoria and Albert Museum**.

MUSEUM CORNER

The V&A is free, but has a voluntary contribution system. Those wishing to enjoy the museum without paying have to walk bravely past the attendants in the boxes in the entrance hall. The system seems to work, but pos-

Brompton Oratory

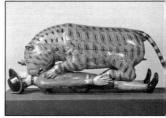

V&A Museum

sibly if too many people go boldly in then an obligatory charge may have to be made. The **Natural History** and **Science Museums**, just around the corner, have adopted charges unless you arrive at 4.30, when they are free until closing time at 6 o'clock (5-6 on Sundays). Time can easily be spent free of charge any day in the V&A until 4.30 and then there is free entry round the

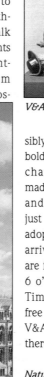

Natural History Museum

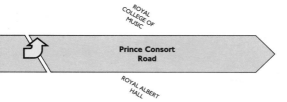

Science Museum

corner. There are free guided tours in the V&A if you have an hour to spare. Wait in the area under the dome for a guide. There is so much to see in the seven miles of galleries that it defies description. All the applied and fine arts are here, not just from Britain but from all over the world, from all cultures and times. The most popular exhibit is the Great Bed of Ware, 12 feet wide – nearly 4 metres – which was famous even as early as Shakespeare's time. The new vaulted restaurant is near the Exhibition Road entrance and a small gallery of Rodin's sculptures.

THE SOUND OF MUSIC

Leaving the V&A in Exhibition Road, cross over to the Science Museum, or, if you plan to skip this, turn north as far as Prince Consort Road. After about a minute the circular shape of the **Royal Albert Hall** is seen on your right up a flight of steps. To your left is the **Royal College of Music**, which has a small museum of musical instruments, although it is primarily a place of study. The Royal Albert Hall is the venue of the summer Promenade Concerts. Great things are planned for the 1990s to refurbish the interior and open up the hall for a wider

ALBERT MEMORIAL

KENSINGTON PALACE

Kensington Road

ROYAL COLLEGE OF ART

variety of events, both daytime and evening. The ornately decorated building to your left, opposite the hall, was the Royal College of Organists for many years and on the

The Royal Albert Hall

corner of the main road the **Royal College of Art** has free exhibitions. Look for the poster on the side of the building.

ALBERT MEMORIAL

Opposite the Royal Albert Hall sits Prince Albert himself, one of the greatest benefactors of London, who died tragically of typhoid fever in 1861. He sponsored the Great Exhibition of 1851 which was held in Hyde Park, just to the east of where he now sits. The exhibition was held in the Crystal Palace, which was itself one of the greatest feats of Victorian engineering, and the exhibits all reflected the latest in Victorian science and technology. The Crystal Palace moved to a site in Sydenham after the exhibition and burnt down in 1936. The book that Albert is holding is one of the catalogues of the Great Exhibition. You may not be able to see Albert if he is still encased in scaffolding for restoration.

A SERPENTINE RAMBLE

Hyde Park, behind the seated prince, shades into Kensington Gardens at some point hereabouts. The nannies are gone now, and mothers have to take their own children to the park, but the bandstand is there, and the Round Pond for model sailing boats. **Kensington Palace** itself has a colourful sunken garden which it is free to peep at, and the Orangery may be open for a polite pot of tea on a fragile garden chair.

SERPENTINE MARBLE ARCH

Knightsbridge

Those people who did not take the advice I gave in Trafalgar Square and who are now pigeons will be pleased to know that the best pickings are to be had in Kensington Gardens. The birds here are so fat that they can hardly take off. Perch on the statue of **Peter Pan** by the **Serpentine** for a quick scratch, then hop around the lake making your way northwards until you reach the Victoria Gate. This is where being a pigeon is useful. Fly over the traffic, keeping Bayswater Road to your left as far as **Marble Arch**. It would take about ten minutes if you had to walk.

TYBURN TREE

Here there is another subway like the one at Hyde Park Corner. Artistically executed mosaics on the walls do not compensate for the faint smell of urine and the menacing atmosphere. If you wish to examine Marble Arch close up there is a certain amount of map reading necessary. The arch was intended to be the entrance to Buckingham Palace but was moved here when it was found that the entrance was too narrow for the Queen's coach. Now it is at the entrance to nowhere and if you have seen the Arc de Triomphe in Paris, do not trouble to inspect this.

The crossroads at Marble Arch is very ancient. Going north from here is Edgware Road. It was built by the

Kensington Palace

Oxford Street

MARBLE ARCH   SPEAKERS CORNER

Romans in the first century AD and later became Watling Street. And from the Middle Ages to 1783 stood here the largest gallows of old London, Tyburn tree, which could hang twenty-four at a time. Stands were erected nearby for spectators. They could also see the grassy place 'where soldiers are shot' according to a map of 1746 – now Speakers Corner. Oxford Street, running east, was once Tyburn Road, where those about to die were pulled on hurdles or carts from Newgate Gaol, and Park Lane was once the rural Tyburn Lane.

If you want to connect up to Walk 1, take a 2A, 2B, 73, 82 or 135 bus to Victoria and then catch an 11, 24, 29, 76, 507, 510 or C1 to the Army and Navy Stores. By tube you need the Central line to Notting Hill Gate, then the Circle or District line to St James's Park.

If you are travelling to London around Christmas and the New Year, please note that most major attractions are closed. A few places are closed on Mondays. Most places in the City are closed on Saturdays and Sundays.

D Attractions with this logo make an effort to welcome the disabled. Other places are accessible with help. Phone for details. See also Disabled in London section. Popular attractions have a queuing system for telephone callers. You lose your place in the queue by re-dialling, so stay on the line.

St Martin-in-the-Fields, Trafalgar Square, WC2
Box office 071-839 1930
U BR Charing Cross
Buses 1, 3, 6, 9, 11, 12, 13, 15, 15B, X15, 24, 29, 53, 53X, 77, 77A, 88, 109, 159, 170, 176, 177Ex, 184, 196
D Phone

National Portrait Gallery, 2 St Martin's Place, WC2
071-306 0055
Free. Mon-Fri 10-5, Sat 10-6, Sun 2-6
U BR Charing Cross
Buses as St Martin-in-the-Fields

National Gallery, Trafalgar Square, WC2
071-839 3321
Free. Mon-Sat 10-6, Sun 2-6
U BR Charing Cross
Buses as St Martin-in-the-Fields
D Orange Street entrance

Institute of Contemporary Arts, The Mall, SW1
Box office 071-930 3647, Recorded information 071-930 6393
Day membership £1.50 max, Under 15 free with an adult
Daily 12-11 pm except Bank Holidays
U Charing Cross
Buses as St Martin-in-the-Fields (no buses go down the Mall)
D Phone

Queen's Gallery, Buckingham Palace Road, SW1
071-930 4832, Recorded information 071-799 2331
Adults £2.00, Children £1.00, Concessions £1.50
Tue-Sat 10-5, Sun 2-5 (last admissions 4.30); closed Mon
except Bank Holidays
No toilets
U St James's Park, Victoria
Buses (to Victoria station) 2, 2A, 2B, 11, 16, 24, 25, 29,
36, 36A, 36B, 38, 39, 52, 52A, 73, 76, 82, 135, 177Ex,
185, 507, 510, C1

Royal Mews, Buckingham Palace Road, SW1
071-930 4832, Recorded information 071-799 2331
Adults £1.30, Senior citizens £1.00, Under 16 70p
Wed & Thur (usually) 12-4 except during Ascot; phone
line gives full details
U St James's Park, Victoria
Buses as Queen's Gallery
D Phone, free

Apsley House, Hyde Park Corner, W1
071-499 5676
Adults £2.00, 5-15 & Concessions £1.00
Tue-Sun 11-5 (last admissions 4.30); closed Mon except
Bank Holidays
U Hyde Park Corner
Buses 2A, 2B, 9, 10, 14, 16, 19, 22, 25, 30, 36, 36B, 38,
52, 52A, 73, 74, 82, 135, 137, 503

Victoria and Albert Museum, Cromwell Road, SW7
071-938 8500, Recorded information 071-938 8441
Donations Adults £3.00, Children & Concessions 50p
Mon-Sat 10-5.50, Sun 2.30-5.50
U South Kensington
Buses 14, 30, 74, 503, C1
D

Science Museum, Exhibition Road, SW7
071-938 8000, Recorded information 071-938 5491
Adults £3.00, Senior citizens £2.00, Children & other
Concessions £1.75
Times as Natural History Museum

U South Kensington
Buses No buses run down Exhibition Road. Get off at V&A
and walk, or take 9, 10, 33, 52, 52A, C1 to Royal Albert
Hall (Queen's Gate)
D

Natural History Museum, Exhibition Road, SW7
Recorded information 042 692 7654
Adults £3.00, 5-18 & Concessions £1.50, Families (2+4
max) £8.00
Mon-Sat 10-6, Sun 1-6
Free Mon-Fri 4.30-6, Sat, Sun & Bank Holidays 5-6
U South Kensington
Buses as Science Museum
D

Geological Museum, now incorporated with Science
Museum

**Royal College of Music, Museum of Instruments,
Prince Consort Road, SW7**
071-589 3643
Adults £1.20, Children & Concessions £1.00
Wednesdays in term time 2-4
U South Kensington
Buses as Science Museum
D Phone

Royal College of Art, Kensington Gore, SW7
071-584 5020
Free. Mon-Fri 10-6
U High Street Kensington, South Kensington
Buses as Royal Albert Hall
D Access, toilet

Royal Albert Hall, SW7
Box office 071-589 8212
U South Kensington
Buses 9, 10, 33, 52, 52A, C1
D Phone

Kensington Palace, W8

071-937 9561
Adults £3.75, Children £2.50, Concessions £2.80,
Families (2+2) £11.00
Mon-Sat 9-5, Sun 1-5 (last admissions 4.15)
U Queensway, High Street Kensington
Buses 9, 10, 33, 49, 52, 52A, C1 to Palace Gate,
Kensington Road
D Phone

FOR THE BEST IN THE
WEST END, FOLLOW THE SIGNS

CREDIT CARD BOOKINGS
071 867 1111

ALBERY THEATRE
St Martin's Lane
London WC2N 4AH
Box Office: 071 837 1115
⊖ Leicester Square

PICCADILLY THEATRE
Denman Street
London W1V 8DY
Box Office: 071 867 1118
⊖ Piccadilly Circus

COMEDY THEATRE
Panton Street
London SW1Y 4DN
Box Office: 071 930 2578
⊖ Piccadilly Circus

WHITEHALL THEATRE
14 Whitehall
London SW1A 2DY
Box Office: 071 867 1119
⊖ Charing Cross

PHOENIX THEATRE
Charing Cross Road
London WC2H OJP
Box Office: 071 240 9661
⊖ Tottenham Court Road

WYNDHAMS THEATRE
Charing Cross Road
London WC2H 0DA
Box Office: 071 867 1116
⊖ Leicester Square

MAYBOX GROUP PLC.
Albery Theatre
St Martin's Lane
London WC2N 4AH
Tel: 071 867 1122
Fax: 071 867 1131

SIDE
TRIPS

WINDSOR
HAMPTON COURT
KEW GARDENS
TATE GALLERY
MUSEUM OF GARDEN
HISTORY
HAMPSTEAD
HOLLAND PARK
CHELSEA
DOCKLANDS

London's motorways and fast, regular coach services have brought many longer distance day trips, which might once have been prohibitively expensive, within the reach of more limited purses.

Victoria coach station is the centre for coaches and enquiries should be made to National Express on 071-730 0202. London Coaches, part of London Transport, operate day coach and river trips and offer longer breaks. See page 129 or phone 071-222 1234 for details.

Windsor, on the Thames, is dominated by one building, the castle. Rising like a fairy-tale castle on its hilltop, the building was founded by William the Conqueror and has been added to by monarchs ever since. The chapel contains the tombs of Henry VIII, Charles I and George III and is decked out with the banners of the Knights of the Garter, one of the oldest orders of chivalry.

Hampton Court, the most beautiful and probably the best loved of England's palaces, was built by Cardinal Wolsey. William and Mary asked Wren to rebuild it to be the Versailles of London but this was not an entire success. The maze is a perennial favourite. Turn left as you go in. You could plan a picnic in the centre of the maze, but I wouldn't bank on finding it before tea-time.

Kew Gardens is only a few miles out of the centre of London. Take the District line to Kew Gardens station and walk the short distance. Plants from all over the world

Windsor Castle

Hampton Court

Hampton Court Maze

share the sprawling lawns with the best of British. It's possible to walk along the river from Kew to Richmond Bridge, where a new riverside frontage development already looks as if it has been there for 200 years. Toil up Richmond Hill for the view of the river from the vantage point. The Star and Garter Home for disabled ex-servicemen where the Remembrance Sunday poppies are made is at the top of the hill. Richmond is also on the District line and both Kew and Richmond can be reached by British Rail from Waterloo.

London Coaches operate trips to Hampton Court and Windsor by river and coach,

Kew Gardens

Richmond Bridge

Richmond Hill

and passenger trips can be booked at Westminster Pier for Kew, Richmond and Hampton Court.

Back in London, but still by the river, the **Tate Gallery** at Millbank offers a stunning collection of modern art alongside more traditional pictures. The collection was founded by the sugar millionaire Henry Tate to be a gallery for British art. The jewel of the collection is Millais' *Ophelia*, floating down the stream. Cross Lambeth Bridge near here to the disused church of St Mary-at-Lambeth. This is not just the burial place of Captain Bligh of the *Bounty*, but of the Tradescants, father and son – once royal gardeners – and the church is now the **Museum of Garden History** (free entry).

London is a collection of villages, from Richmond in the west to the alpine village of Beckton in the east (its 'alp' is a dry ski slope on an old slag heap). The most favoured of these is Hampstead. It has a villagey atmosphere, tea shops and pubs, **Keats' House** (where he wrote 'Ode to a Nightingale'), **Kenwood** (the Iveagh Bequest) and the heath. From Parliament Hill on the edge of the heath the whole of London is spread before your feet.

London's open spaces provide much in the way of free entertainment. See Traditional events section for details of

Hampstead

Druids on Primrose Hill, veteran vehicles at Crystal Palace and Punch and Judy festivals at Covent Garden (although this isn't quite an open space). **Holland Park** has grounds that bring the countryside into the town, and the house is now a youth hostel – combine it with a visit to Portobello Road nearby (see Markets section). If you visit Chelsea for the Flower Show, stop and explore the village. It's also possible to see round the **Royal Hospital** and Museum at certain times of the week, guided by the Chelsea Pensioners. This is completely free.

London's newest village – if that is the right name for it – is **Docklands,** and for the price of a Travelcard the whole of the Docklands Light Railway system is yours as well as the rest of London. Just get on at Tower Gateway, near Tower Hill tube station, and explore. Island Gardens is the stop for Greenwich, connected by a leaky foot

Docklands

tunnel. Greenwich has the **National Maritime Museum**, *Cutty Sark* and *Gypsy Moth IV*, and the village itself can be explored quite inexpensively.

Gypsy Moth IV

Cutty Sark

National Maritime Museum

Windsor Castle, Windsor, Berks

Precincts: Daily except 14 June from 10.30. Closing times
vary with daylight. For full details telephone Windsor
0753 868286
(Further details about Windsor from Tourist Information
Centre 0753 852010)
BR Windsor (from Waterloo)

Hampton Court Palace

081-977 8441
Admission to palace and maze: Adults £4.50, 5-15 £2.80,
Concessions £3.40, Families £13.50
April to October daily 9.30-5.30 (last admissions)
October to March last admissions at 4.
Park open 7 am to dusk daily
BR Hampton Court from Waterloo
Buses 715, 718
D

Royal Botanical Gardens, Kew

081-940 1171
Adults £3.00, 5-15 £1.00, Concessions £1.50
Daily from 9.30, closing time varies with daylight
U Kew Gardens
BR Kew Bridge (from Waterloo)
Buses 7, 27
D

Tate Gallery, Millbank, SW1

071-821 1313, Recorded information 071-821 7128
Free. Mon-Sat 10-5.50, Sun 2-5.50
U Pimlico
Buses 3, 76, 77A, 159, 507, 510
D

Museum of Garden History, St Mary-at-Lambeth, Lambeth Palace Road, SE1

071-261 1891
Free. Mon-Fri 11-3, Sun 10.30-5
U Lambeth North
Buses 3, 44, 76, 77, 159, 170, 507, 510
D

Keats' House, Keats' Grove, NW3
071-435 2062
Free. April to October Mon-Fri 2-6, Sat 10-1, 2-5, Sun 2-5
including Bank Holidays; November to March Mon-Fri
1-5, weekends as summer, closed winter Bank Holidays
U Hampstead then a pleasant walk through the village
Buses (to Hampstead) 24, 46, 168, 268

Kenwood House (the Iveagh Bequest), Hampstead Lane, NW3
081-348 1286
Free. Easter to September daily 10-6, September to Easter
10-4
U Not very convenient for Golders Green, Hampstead or
Highgate, some parking
Bus 210 from Archway tube station on the Northern line
D Limited

Holland Park, W8
071-602 9483
U Holland Park, High Street Kensington
Buses (to Commonwealth Institute) 9, 10, 27, 28, 31, 33, 49
(to Notting Hill Gate from Oxford Street) 12, 88

Royal Hospital Chelsea and Museum, Royal Hospital Road, SW3
071-730 0161
Free. April to September Mon-Sat 10-12, 2-4; October to
March Sun 2-4 (museum closed in winter on Sunday
afternoons)
U Sloane Square
Buses 11, 19, 22, 39, 137

Royal Horticultural Society, Vincent Square, SW1
Recorded information 071-828 1744 for details of Chelsea
Flower Show, seasonal shows and competitions.

Cutty Sark, King William Walk, SE10
081-858 3445
Adults £2.50, Under 16 & Concessions £1.25 (children
must be with an adult), Families (2+5 max) £6.00
April to September Mon-Sat 10-6, Sun 12-6;

October to March closes at 5
BR Greenwich, Maze Hill (from London Bridge)
DLR to Island Gardens then foot tunnel
Buses 1, 177, 188

Gypsy Moth IV, King William Walk, SE10
081-853 3445
Adults 50p, Under 16 30p
Easter to October daily 10-5.30 (last admissions); closed winter
BR Greenwich, Maze Hill (from London Bridge)
DLR Island Gardens then foot tunnel
Buses 1, 177, 188

London Docklands Development Corporation Visitors' Centre, Limeharbour, Isle of Dogs
071-515 3000, ask for Visitors' Centre
Open daily
DLR Crossharbour, South Quays (Limeharbour runs north from the eastern end of Crossharbour and is also the site of the London Arena, a 12,000-seat sports and entertainment venue)
Local buses D5, D6, P14

Docklands Light Railway
071-222 1234

STREET MARKETS

London is rightly famed for its bustling street markets where you can buy anything from Georgian silver to a couple of apples for lunch. Some sell mainly food, others specialise. There are still bargains to be found, but fewer than there used to be.

New Caledonian Market, Bermondsey Square, SE1
Antiques. Fridays – early morning (dealers trade before 7 am!)
U Elephant and Castle then buses 1, 188
Buses 1, 42, 78, 188

Camden Lock, Camden NW1
Saturdays and Sundays. Crafts, bric-à-brac, antiques in an

attractive canalside setting.
U Camden Town then a short walk. This is not a million
miles from Regent's Park.
Buses (to Camden Town) 24, 27, 29, 31, 46, 68, 74, 134,
135, 168, 214, 253, C2

Camden Passage, Islington High Street, N1
Antiques and bric-à-brac. Wednesdays and Saturdays.
(This is not near Camden Lock.)
U Angel
Buses (to the Angel) 4, 19, 30, 38, 43, 56, 73, 153, 171,
171A, 196, 214, 263A, 279, 279A

Chapel Market, White Conduit Street, N1
Food and household. Tuesdays to Sunday mornings. (This is
just across the main road from Camden Passage going west.)
U Angel
Buses as to Camden Passage

Covent Garden, WC2
General, antiques on Mondays. Daily except Sunday.
U Covent Garden
Buses (along the Strand) 1, 6, 9, 11, 13, 15, 15B, X15,
77, 77A , 170, 176, 177 Ex, 196; (down Charing Cross
Road) 24, 29, 176

Leadenhall Market, Gracechurch Street, EC3
Food, especially fish. Mondays to Fridays office hours.
U Bank then walk along Cornhill to Gracechurch Street.
The market is behind the buildings; look for an alley.
Buses 15B, 22A, 25, 35, 47, 48, 505

Leather Lane, Holborn, EC1
General. Mondays to Fridays 11-2. This street runs
parallel to Hatton Garden, the street of the diamond
merchants.
U Chancery Lane. It's not always easy to tell which way
you're facing when you come out of this tube station. You
need to have the black and white building of Staple Inn
on your right. Leather Lane is a small turning on your left.
Buses 8, 17, 18, 22B, 25, 45, 46, 171A, 243, 259, 501

Petticoat Lane, Middlesex Street, E1

Clothes, food, novelties. Sunday mornings (9 am or earlier).

U Liverpool Street, Aldgate (It's easier to find from Aldgate as Liverpool Street has several exits.)

Buses 5, 15, 15B, X15, 25, 40, 42, 44, 67, 78, 100, 253, 510

Portobello Road, Notting Hill, W11

Antiques, junk, fruit, general. Mondays to Saturdays.

U Notting Hill Gate, then go north up Pembridge Villas and take second left.

Buses 7, 15, 27, 28, 31, 52A (ask for Westbourne Grove)

Portobello Road

EVENINGS OUT

A night out in London can cost you as much – or as little – as you want to spend. For value for money the immense variety of pubs with their songs, shows and characters – and often histories as well – is almost impossible to beat (as is a smoky atmosphere).

It's easy to sit all evening over a glass of *vin français* at the Café des Amis du Vin in Hanover Place. This basement wine bar is near Covent Garden tube station and has proper tables on the ground floor for more formal meals. The staff are relaxed and French. Or try the Cafe Pacifico, off Long Acre, for Mexican food and sangria in a converted warehouse, or the Rock Garden for burgers and rock – all in the Covent Garden area.

The crime buff might prefer a quieter drink at the Sherlock Holmes pub in Northumberland Avenue. This is quite near Charing Cross station and not far from the Playhouse theatre, which belongs to novelist and politician Jeffrey Archer. Insomniacs can try Harry's all-night cafe in Kingly Street. This is just behind Regent Street round the back of Liberty's department store.

If you want to walk and talk you might find yourselves down by the river. The south side of the Thames is pretty quiet, except for the South Bank arts centre area. Try the pubs I sent you to in Walk 3, the George and the Anchor. There are other waterside pubs to explore on the north side of the river – the Dickens at St Katharine's Dock or the Town of Ramsgate and the Prospect of Whitby at Wapping. These can be reached on foot from St Katharine's Dock. Just keep the river on your right and stick as close to the water as possible. Or you could join one of the guided evening walks which take in these pubs. Get the weeklies like *What's On*, *City Limits* and *Time Out* for details.

To travel on the water itself on a fine summer evening, phone Charing Cross Pier on 071-839 3572 for up-to-date details of their 45-minute evening cruises.

For cheap theatre tickets queue at the booth in Leicester Square for half-price tickets for that night's performance. The booth is no fly-by-night operation (as its flimsy structure might suggest) but is run by the Society of West End Theatre.

"THE GREATEST MUSICAL OF THE DECADE"

Sheridan Morley • Punch & International Herald Tribune

WILLY RUSSELL'S
AWARD WINNING MUSICAL

BLOOD
Brothers

"STANDS HEAD AND SHOULDERS ABOVE EVERY OTHER SHOW IN TOWN"
BBC Radio

ALBERY THEATRE
— St. Martins Lane • WC2 —
BOX OFFICE & CREDIT CARDS: 071 867 1115

WEST END TICKETS

14 CHARING CROSS ROAD, LONDON WC2

071 240 2337 10 lines
FAX 071 836 5049

WE OBTAIN THE UNOBTAINABLE TICKETS

"MISS SAIGON"
"ASPECTS OF LOVE"
"LES MISERABLES"
"CATS"
"PHANTOM OF THE OPERA"

AND ALL WEST END SHOWS

ALSO ALL SPORTING EVENTS
WIMBLEDON   F.A.CUP   CRICKET
HENLEY REGATTA   ROYAL ASCOT

ALL CONCERTS
WEMBLEY   HAMMERSMITH,
LONDON ARENA   ALBERT HALL

FREE DELIVERY THROUGHOUT CENTRAL LONDON

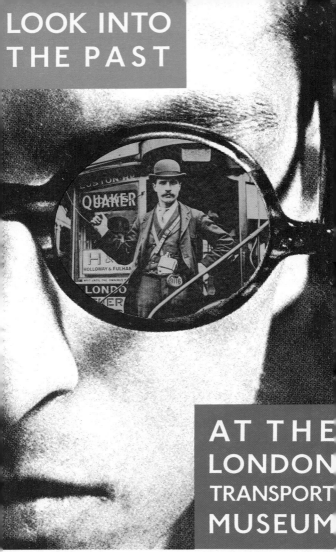

LOOK INTO THE PAST

AT THE LONDON TRANSPORT MUSEUM

Browse among our unique collection of historic vehicles, posters and archive film.

Put yourself in the driving seat of a London bus or Underground train.

Visit the Museum Shop for the best selection of reproduction posters in town.

Open Daily 10.00-18.00. (Last admission 17.15).
Museum closed 24/25/26 Dec. Phone 071-379 6344
071-836 8557 24 hr. information.
How to get there: *Underground:* Covent Garden or
Leicester Square *British Rail:* Charing Cross.
Bus: Any bus to Aldwych or Strand.

London Transport Museum, The Piazza, Covent Garden, London WC2E 7BB.

TRADITIONAL EVENTS

The London Tourist Board (LTB) publishes a list of traditional events each January to help plan your trip to the capital. Phone LTB on 071-730 3488 for exact dates. For events in the City call in or phone the information bureau in St Paul's Churchyard on 071-606 3030. Acknowledgements to LTB for supplying the information below (in October 1990). Note that all guidebooks are out of date in some respects by the time they appear, so do check with the relevant tourist body before setting out.

DAILY

Changing the guard: Horse guards leave their barracks in Hyde Park 10.28 am Mon-Sat, 9.28 am Sun, for the ceremony at Horse Guards, Whitehall, at 11 am Mon-Sat, 10 am Sun. Changing the guard at Buckingham Palace is 11.30 daily April to end July and alternate days from August to approximately end March (not in wet weather).

NIGHTLY

Ceremony of the Keys: Tower. Write for tickets to the Governor, Tower of London, EC3N 4AB, with as many alternative dates as possible.

JANUARY

Royal Epiphany Gifts Service: 6 January at Chapel Royal, St James's Palace, SW1.

Charles I Commemoration: Last Sunday at Banqueting House and Trafalgar Square, midday.

FEBRUARY

Chinese New Year: Dates vary for celebrations in Soho. Gun salute: 6 February. Commemorates Queen's accession to throne. Hyde Park at noon, Tower at 1 pm. (If 6 February is a Sunday, guns are fired on following Monday.)

MARCH

Oxford and Cambridge University Boat Race: On a Saturday on the Thames between Putney Bridge and Mortlake.

Bridewell Thanksgiving Service: Second Tuesday at St Bride's church, Fleet Street. Lord Mayor of London, in robes, attends service at noon.

Oranges and Lemons Service: Third or fourth Thursday at church of St Clement Danes in the Strand, 3 pm.

Spring Equinox: Druids celebrate the equinox on Tower Hill at noon.

EASTER

Maundy Money: In 1991 this ceremony is at Westminster Abbey, but it moves to a different place each year.

Butterworth Charity: Morning service at St Bartholomew-the-Great, Smithfield, concludes with distribution of money and hot cross buns.

Easter Parade: Easter Sunday in Battersea Park.

Harness Horse Parade: Easter Monday in Regent's Park.

APRIL

Spital Sermon: First Thursday after Easter at St Lawrence Jewry-next-Guildhall. Lord Mayor, sheriffs, aldermen in procession from Guildhall, noon.

Stow Commemoration: St Andrew Undershaft, Leadenhall Street, EC3. Date varies.

Gun salute: 21 April, Queen's birthday (as February).

Tyburn Walk: Silent procession from Old Bailey to Marble Arch, last Sunday.

MAY

Historic Commercial Vehicle Run: First Sunday at Crystal Palace Park from 6.30 am.

Epsom Derby: First Wednesday on Epsom Downs, Surrey.

Dunkirk Veterans' Service: St Lawrence Jewry-next-Guildhall, EC2, 3pm. Date varies.

London Private Fire Brigades' target spraying competition: Guildhall Yard, noon on a May Saturday, also on a date in September.

Punch and Judy Festival: Covent Garden, followed by service at St Paul's, Covent Garden, second Sunday at 11 am.

Beating the Bounds: All Hallows-by-the-Tower, Ascension Day (sixth Thursday after Easter), 3 pm.

Every three years also at St Peter ad Vincula in the Tower, 6 pm.

Chelsea Flower Show: Late May at the Royal Hospital, Chelsea. Phone 071-828 1744 for recorded details.

JUNE

Trooping the Colour: Second Sunday in June to celebrate the Queen's official birthday. Horse Guards Parade, 11 am. Write for a maximum of two tickets before the end of February to the Brigade Major (Trooping the Colour), Headquarters, Household Division, Horse Guards, SW1A 2AX.

Beating Retreat and Sounding Retreat: In June on Horse Guards Parade. Tickets from the end of February from Premier Box Office, 1b Bridge Street, SW1A 2JR, 071-839 6815/071-836 4114.

Royal Ascot: Towards the end of June. Tickets from the Secretary, Grandstand, Ascot, Berks.

Gun salute: 10 June for birthday of Prince Philip. See February for details.

Pepys Commemoration Service: St Olave's church, Hart Street, EC3R 7NB. Write to the church for details of the service and the buffet lunch.

Election of sheriffs: Around midsummer at Guildhall. Write in advance for tickets to the Keeper, Guildhall, EC2P 2EJ.

JULY

Royal Tournament: Mid-July at Earl's Court. The Queen and other senior members of the Royal Family take the salute. Write from mid-March to Royal Tournament Box Office, Earl's Court Exhibition Centre, Warwick Road, SW5 9TA.

Royal Tournament

AUGUST

Gun salute: 4 August for the Queen Mother's birthday. See February for details.

Cart Marking Ceremony: Guildhall Yard at midday.

London Riding Horse Parade: First Sunday in August, Rotten Row. Phone LTB for the address of the current secretary of the parade to obtain entry form and details.

Notting Hill Carnival: August Bank Holiday and the Sunday before it.

SEPTEMBER

Autumn Equinox: Druids hold equinox celebrations at Primrose Hill.

Election of Lord Mayor: 29 September, or near, at Guildhall. Tickets from the Keeper, Guildhall, EC2P 2EJ.

Punch and Judy Festival: Covent Garden.

OCTOBER

Judges' Service: First weekday in October, Westminster Abbey. Private function but procession to Parliament at about 11.45.

Pearly Harvest Festival: First Sunday at St Martin-in-the-Fields, Trafalgar Square, 3 pm.

Vintage Festival: St Olave's, Hart Street, EC3.

Harvest of the Sea: Second Sunday in October at either St Mary-at-Hill, EC3, or St Margaret Pattens, Rood Lane.

National Service for Seafarers: Nearest Wednesday to Trafalgar Day, 21 October, St Paul's Cathedral, 6 pm. Tickets from Hon. Sec., Annual National Service for Seafarers, St Michael Paternoster Royal, College Hill, EC4R 2RL.

NOVEMBER

Fireworks Night: Yeomen of the Guard still check the cellars of the Houses of Parliament prior to the State Opening of Parliament and all around the country bonfires and firework displays are held on or near 5 November.

Phone 071-730 3488 in October for London firework displays.

State Opening of Parliament: Early to mid-November. Not open to public but usually on television. Procession from Buckingham Palace at approximately 11 am.

London to Brighton Veteran Car Run: First Sunday in November. Starts Hyde Park Corner 8-9 am.

Lord Mayor's Show: Second Saturday of November. Procession in City from 11 am.

Remembrance Sunday Ceremony: Second Sunday in November, Cenotaph, Whitehall, 11 am.

DECEMBER

Boar's Head Presentation: Procession to Mansion House, in the City. Date varies.

CHRISTMAS

Christmas lights: Switched on in Regent Street and Oxford Street in mid-November.

New Year's Eve: Midnight in crowded Trafalgar Square, or Parliament Square to hear Big Ben ring in the new year.

Christmas lights

Bank Holidays	1991	1992
New Year's Day	1 January	1 January
Good Friday	29 March	17 April
Easter Monday	1 April	20 April
May Day Bank Holiday	6 May	4 May
Spring Bank Holiday	27 May	25 May
August Bank Holiday	26 August	31 August
Christmas Day	25 December	25 December
Boxing Day	26 December	28 December

USING LONDON'S PUBLIC TRANSPORT

When you visit London, the best way to get around is the Londoners' way – by public transport. Central London and the suburbs are well served by both bus and Underground networks, and the fully wheelchair accessible Docklands Light Railway has opened up the Thames-side areas east of the Tower.

The headquarters of London Transport (LT) is at 55 Broadway, SW1, above St James's Park tube station, which also houses the London Transport Travel Shop. This deals not only with tickets and London Transport enquiries but sells a wide range of LT merchandise, souvenirs and books. In addition, there are Travel Information Centres at the following Underground stations: St James's Park, King's Cross, Liverpool Street, Oxford Circus, Piccadilly Circus and Heathrow. There are other LT Travel Information Centres at Victoria station and Euston British Rail station, at West Croydon bus station and at all Heathrow terminals. See the London Transport services section for further details. Phone 071-222 1234 for travel enquiries and Travelcheck on 071-222 1200 for regularly updated travel information.

UNDERGROUND

The **Underground**, or tube, is the most comprehensive subway network in the world. It's fast and convenient – unless you're in a wheelchair. If this is the case see Disabled in London section for advice on transport in London. There are eleven Underground lines including the Docklands Light Railway, each with its own colour code. See the journey planner on the back cover. Smoking is banned everywhere on the Underground system.

DOCKLANDS LIGHT RAILWAY

The **Docklands Light Railway** (DLR) was opened in 1987, and runs in a Y-shape from Tower Gateway and Stratford down to a terminus at Island Gardens on the Isle of Dogs, where there is a DLR visitor centre. Extensions are planned to Bank in the City and to Beckton, beyond the eastern Royal Docks.

The service is fully automated with trains running

every few minutes. The main station is at Tower Gateway where there is a small information office (open 10–4 Mon–Fri only). Ticket machines take coins rather than notes so be sure to have plenty of change. Travelcards are valid on the service (see opposite for details).

BUSES

Buses are no longer all red but those that aren't can be recognised as part of the London Transport system by the familiar roundel that they all carry. If you are sightseeing you may not want to go the fastest way, by tube, choosing instead to catch some sights on the way. Buses to the central attractions covered in this book are indicated in the in-

dividual chapters. If you take the number 11, for example, it will take you from Liverpool Street station through the City, past St Paul's, Trafalgar Square, Westminster Abbey and down the King's Road to Chelsea. Or try the number 188 from Euston, which goes to Greenwich via the British Museum and the South Bank arts complex, and passes close to Tower Bridge. Free bus maps and guides are obtainable at LT's Travel Information Centres.

Buses have their own intriguing history. For instance, the bottom deck of a double-decker is still called 'inside', recalling the days when the top was open to the weather. See the London Transport Museum in Covent Garden for their fascinating collection of historic vehicles, posters and memorabilia.

Most **bus stops** in central London are named on the

post or shelter and carry travel information. There are two kinds of stops: the compulsory stop, red on a white background, and the request stop, white on a red background. To hail the bus put out an arm. The driver will not stop if the bus is full. Sometimes it's wise to hail a bus at the compulsory stop, especially at night, in case the driver hasn't seen you.

Buses with a conductor are double-deckers (usually boarded at the back) and the conductor will tell you where to get off if you ask. Ring the bell in good time just once to tell the driver to stop. Driver-only-operated buses (both single- and double-deckers) are boarded at the front.

Red Arrows are single-deck buses (501-513) running mainly between British Rail stations. They are driver-operated buses with a flat fare, currently 70p. Exact money is needed and the driver cannot give change.

Carelink and **Mobility** Buses are run by LT for the disabled, see Disabled in London section for details.

Night buses all pass through Trafalgar Square and serve main cinema, restaurant and theatre areas in central London until the day buses start. They have an N in front of the route number. For full details phone 071-222 1234.

BUYING YOUR TICKET

One-journey bus tickets are bought on the bus and one-journey single or return tickets on the tube are bought at the station of departure. Keep your ticket until the end of the journey in case an inspector is travelling on your route.

London is divided into six travel zones, from zone 1 in the central area to zone 6 in the suburbs. Bus passes are available in different combinations of zones for a week, a month or three months. They are valid at any time of day and are used by London's commuters. Buy them from certain bus garages, selected newsagents and Travel Information Centres. You will need to take a passport-type photograph along with you.

One-day, 7-day, monthly and 3-monthly Travelcards are valid for bus, Mobility Bus, tube and DLR, and for

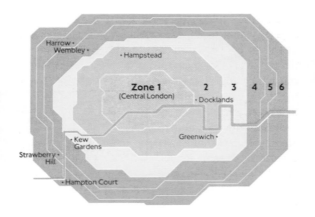

Network SouthEast (the British Rail suburban system). They are not valid on the Airbus or on guided coach tours. The 1-day Travelcards are valid after 9.30 am on Mondays to Fridays, and all day at weekends. They are not valid on the night buses. Travelcards are for sale at tube stations, Travel Information Centres and some newsagents. For all Travelcards except the 1-day you will need to present a passport-type photo when you buy.

AUTOMATIC MACHINES

There are self-service **ticket machines** in most tube stations to save a long wait. Follow the instructions on the machines. The larger style of machine displays the prices and zones. The smaller machine can be used if you know the fare. Both types accept coins from the 5p piece to the £1 and give change. The larger machine accepts the £5 note in good condition. Be sure to keep plenty of change to hand. **Ticket gates** are also automated. To enter the tube system slide the

ticket with the wording uppermost into the slot on the right-hand side of the gate. The gate opens when you remove your ticket. Leave the station in the same way – the ticket is returned to you if it is valid for another journey.

GETTING TO THE AIRPORT

The wheelchair accessible **Airbus** links the major hotel areas with **Heathrow** every half-hour from approximately 6.30 am until 8 pm. The tube (Piccadilly line) also links central London with Heathrow, and the journey takes about an hour. At night, bus N97 runs hourly between central London and Heathrow.

Gatwick is served by the Gatwick Express from Victoria British Rail station every 15 minutes from 5.30 am to 10 pm. The journey time is 30 minutes non-stop. Less frequent trains run overnight. You can check your luggage in at Victoria for some flights from Gatwick; ring first to find out (0293 31299).

DISABLED IN LONDON

It is possible to see many of the sights of London with careful advance planning. Most major museums and tourist attractions are improving their facilities for the disabled all the time and welcome wheelchairs, especially if you telephone first. Madame Tussaud's have to limit the number of wheelchairs they permit in case of fire, so do phone there before you set out. Phone numbers are given in the information sections for each itinerary.

Getting into London from Heathrow is not difficult by wheelchair as there are frequent wheelchair accessible **Airbuses** from Heathrow to Victoria and Euston stations that stop at several hotels on routes A1 and A2. Phone London Transport (LT) on 071-222 1234 for travel information. Leave out the 071 prefix if you are dialling from a number that has an 071 prefix.

The clockwise **Carelink** wheelchair bus run by LT runs hourly every day and connects up seven main railway termini: Euston, St Pancras, King's Cross, Liverpool Street, Waterloo, Victoria and Paddington. The driver may be able to make extra stops with advance notice as long as the timetable can be kept to. Phone LT's Unit for Disabled Passengers on 071-222 5600 for further information.

LT run **Mobility Buses** regularly to help the disabled in the suburbs do their shopping. Standard bus fares are charged as if the service were a regular bus. The most useful bus for visitors is Route 925 which runs on Wednesdays only from the East End. It arrives at Tower Gateway at 10.20 and stops at Liverpool Street, King's Cross, Euston, Oxford Circus, Marble Arch, Hyde Park Corner and Victoria station (at 11.40). The return trip leaves the Wilton Road coach station (Victoria) at 13.45 and arrives back at Liverpool Street at 15.00 before heading out to the East End. Phone 071-222 5600 for details.

The **Original London Transport Sightseeing Tour** has special wheelchair accessible tours from Wilton Road coach station (Victoria) on Saturdays, Mondays and Thursdays. Phone 071-828 7395 for information and booking.

The **Docklands Light Railway** (DLR) is completely automated with trains that are fully accessible for wheelchairs (two per train). An emergency button on the trains and platforms connects with the control room in case of difficulties. Automatic ticket machines take coins rather than notes, so be sure to have plenty of change on you. Travelcards are valid on the DLR as it is part of LT. Note that the 925 Mobility Bus stops at Tower Gateway DLR station on Wednesdays. Travel enquiries on the usual LT number 071-222 1234 (queuing system so hang on); leaflets from 071-222 5600.

The **Underground** is the least preferred option by wheelchair users and non-folding wheelchairs cannot be accommodated at all times on many sections. LT publish *Access to the Underground* to help, but steps are everywhere.

Disabled **car parking** is available in several places on the outer edges of inner London. Phone *Tripscope* on 081-994 9294 in office hours for free information on getting around anywhere in London. There are several useful phone numbers for the disabled in London (see below for a selection), but with the charity *Tripscope* you tap into the 'disability mafia' – the network of London disabled who know all the wheezes and short cuts because they live here.

Roving **taxis** are becoming more and more wheelchair accessible, especially from ranks where the adapted cabs are more easily spotted. If you are unlucky try the following numbers and ask for a taxi which can take a wheelchair, giving as much notice as possible:

Black Radio Taxis	081-209 0266
Data Cab	071-727 7200
Computer Cab	071-286 7009
Lords Radio Taxis	071-253 5000
Radio Taxis	071-272 0272

or phone *Tripscope* (who kindly provided these numbers) for an up-to-date list.

An independent guide to getting around London is *Access in London*, published by Nicholson in 1989, which has details of steps and toilets and much more.

For a RADAR key to disabled toilets and other information phone in office hours or write to the Royal Association for Disability and Rehabilitation (RADAR), 25 Mortimer Street, W1, 071-637 5400.

Other useful numbers are: Disabled Living Foundation, 071-289 6111; Greater London Association for the Disabled (GLAD), 071-274 0107; Disability Action Westminster, 071-630 5994; and Artsline (for arts and entertainment access), 071-388 2227.

LT's Unit for Disabled Passengers will send a comprehensive package of up-to-date London Transport information (in large print or on cassette if wished). Phone 071-222 5600 in office hours or write to them at 55 Broadway, SW1H 0BD. The London Transport Museum, in the corner of Covent Garden, is fully accessible for wheelchairs, with free admission for the disabled and their helpers.

LONDON TRANSPORT SERVICES

The **Travel Information Service** is London Transport's shop window. It exists to provide passengers and potential passengers with helpful advice and guidance about every aspect of travelling around London – by bus, by tube, by the Docklands Light Railway and by British Rail. It can also give general information about the London tourist scene. Details of the location and opening times of Travel Information Centres are given below. Alternatively ring 071-222 1234.

TRAVEL INFORMATION CENTRES

These are open at Underground stations, Heathrow Airport and West Croydon bus station as follows:

	Mon-Fri	Saturday	Sunday
Euston	07.15-18.00	07.15-18.00	08.15-18.00
(BR Concourse)	(to 19.30 Fri)		
King's Cross	08.15-18.00	08.15-18.00	08.15-18.00
	(to 19.30 Fri)		
Liverpool Street	09.30-18.30	08.30-18.30	08.30-15.30
Oxford Circus	08.15-18.00	08.15-18.00	CLOSED
Piccadilly Circus	08.15-18.00	08.15-18.00	08.15-18.00
St James's Park	09.00-17.30	CLOSED	CLOSED
Victoria	08.15-21.30	08.15-21.30	08.15-21.30

(BR Concourse – opposite Platform 8)

Heathrow 1,2,3 (station)
	Mon-Fri	Saturday	Sunday
	07.15-18.30	07.15-18.30	08.15-18.30

Heathrow Terminal 1
| | 07.15-22.15 | 07.15-21.00 | 08.15-22.00 |

Heathrow Terminal 2
| | 07.15-21.00 | 07.15-21.00 | 08.15-22.00 |

Heathrow Terminal 3
| | 06.30-13.15 | 06.30-13.15 | 08.15-15.00 |

Heathrow Terminal 4
| | 06.30-18.30 | 06.30-18.30 | 08.15-18.30 |

West Croydon bus station
Mon 07.00-19.00, Tue-Fri 07.30-18.30, Sat 08.00-18.30, Sun closed

24-hour travel information: 071-222 1234

Travelcheck recorded information: 071-222 1200

For information by post, write to Travel Information Service, London Transport, 55 Broadway, London SW1H 0BD.

Free maps and leaflets Tourist information folders and Underground maps, along with a range of other free leaflets, are available at Travel Information Centres and most hotels.

Bargain Tickets and Tourist Services Ask at Underground stations and Travel Information Centres for prices and availability of Travelcards and bus passes.

The Original London Transport Sightseeing Tour and **Official guided coach tours** See page 128 and ask for free leaflets at Travel Information Centres.

London Transport Museum, The Piazza, Covent Garden; open daily except 24, 25 and 26 December 10 am to 6 pm (last admission 5.15 pm). Come and see the many colourful and historic displays including horse buses, motor buses, trams, trolleybuses and railway vehicles. The museum shop (entrance free) stocks a wide range of books, posters, postcards and unusual souvenirs.

USING THE TELEPHONE

Central London numbers begin with the prefix 071- and outer London numbers begin with 081-. Central London is the area within four miles of Charing Cross. You do not need to dial the prefix if the number you are phoning from already has the same prefix. If you have any difficulty dial 100 and the operator will help you.

Phone boxes take 10p, 20p, 50p and £1 coins and the display tells you to 'insert coin' before you begin to dial. Unused coins are returned. Some phone boxes take phonecards only. These can be bought from post offices and newsagents' shops and cost £2, £4, £10 and £20. If you want directory enquiries dial 142 for London postal addresses and 192 for other British addresses. If you are phoning abroad dial 190 for general enquiries or 153 for directory enquiries. The direct dialling code out of Britain begins 010-.

Some telephone boxes now take credit cards. Instructions are displayed in the individual boxes.

HELP IN AN EMERGENCY

For emergencies dial 999 for police, fire brigade or ambulance. The call is free from any telephone.

Bliss chemists at Marble Arch are open till midnight every day of the week. Their telephone number is 071-723 6116.

British Transport Police, for reporting crimes on London Transport, are on 071-222 5600.

If you need hospital treatment in central London try University College Hospital, Gower Street, WC1; Middlesex Hospital, Mortimer Street, W1; St Mary's Hospital, Praed Street, W2; St Thomas' Hospital, Lambeth Palace Road, SE1, or Westminster Hospital, Horseferry Road, SW1.

Emergency dental treatment can be obtained at a charge from the Emergency Dental Service, 081-677 6363.

Property lost on buses or tubes may find its way to the Lost Property Office at 200 Baker Street, NW1 5RZ, near Baker Street tube station. The office is open on Mondays to Fridays 9.30 to 2 pm. For lost property recorded information ring 071-486 2496. For other lost property apply to the nearest police station.

TOURIST INFORMATION

London Tourist Board and Convention Bureau
26 Grosvenor Gardens, SW1W 0DU, 071-730 3450

Information centres at:
Victoria station Forecourt
SW1: open Easter to October daily 9-8.30 pm; November
to Easter Mon-Sat 9-7 pm, Sun 9-5 pm

Harrods
Knightsbridge, SW1 (fourth floor): open during store
hours

Heathrow Airport
Terminals 1, 2, 3, Underground station Concourse: open
daily 9-6 pm; Terminal 2 Arrivals Concourse, open daily
9-7 pm

Selfridges
Oxford Street, W1 (Basement Services Arcade); open
during store hours

Tower of London
West Gate, EC3; open Easter to October daily 10-6 pm

Telephone information service
071-730 3488 Mon-Fri 9-6 pm (automatic queuing
system)

British Travel Centre
12 Regent Street, Piccadilly Circus, SW1Y 4PQ,
071-730 3400: open Mon-Fri 9-6.30 pm, Sat & Sun 10-4
pm (extended in summer)

City of London Information Centre
St Paul's Churchyard, EC4, 071-606 3030, for
information relating to the square mile of the City of
London: open May to September daily 9.30-5 pm;
October to April Mon-Fri 9.30-5 pm, Sat 9.30-12 noon.

Bureaux de Change
Banks are normally open Mon-Fri 9.30-3.30 pm. Other
exchange facilities can be found at mainline railway
stations, central Underground stations and in some larger
department stores. They may have longer opening hours
than banks.

THE ORIGINAL LONDON TRANSPORT
SIGHTSEEING TOUR

Take an introductory look at London with the Original
London Transport Sightseeing Tour – open top in good
weather. You pass all the major central London attractions:
Tower Bridge, Tower, St Paul's Cathedral, Piccadilly Circus, Trafalgar Square, Houses of Parliament and Big Ben,
travelling along some of London's famous streets: Fleet
Street, Strand, Park Lane and around Hyde Park Corner.

Guided tours in English go from Piccadilly Circus
(Haymarket, Stop L), Victoria station (Victoria Street, Stop
T) and Marble Arch (Park Lane, Stop Z) every 30 minutes
daily from 10 am until 4 pm (except at 1.30 pm).

A tour with taped commentary in English, Dutch,
French, German, Italian, Japanese, Spanish and Swedish
leaves the forecourt of Baker Street Underground station at
the same times. Note that the times shown are only a
guide and are subject to alteration to meet demand. Where
possible, the departures on the hour are maintained.

Combined tickets to save queuing at Madame Tussaud's,
London Zoo and Rock Circus are available from sales agents
listed below and from departure points, except that the
Madame Tussaud's ticket is not sold at Baker Street:

- Porters' desks at many hotels
- London Coaches Wilton Road coach station, Victoria
- London Transport Travel Information Centres
- London Tourist Board Information Centres
- American Express Desk at the British Travel Centre,
  12 Regent Street W1.

Tours information

071-227 3456.
For wheelchair accessible tours see the Disabled in
London section or phone 071-828 7395.

OFFICIAL GUIDED COACH TOURS

Because London Transport knows the best way to see the
sights, they have assembled an exciting programme of
guided tours, carefully selected to show you places that
have played an important part in England's history.

On each tour you travel in a modern luxury coach and

are escorted by a friendly and experienced guide who has an expert knowledge of the places you will visit, and is approved to the high standard of the London Tourist Board.

A London Transport guided tour is a wonderful day out. On each day tour you can enjoy a relaxing lunch, and the price of all tours includes admissions charges.

SUMMER PROGRAMME
London Tours
Day tours
Westminster and City including changing of the guard and the Tower; river tour to Hampton Court Palace.

Morning tours
Westminster and changing of the guard.

Sunday luncheon cruise
Sights of London/changing of the guard/lunch cruising to Greenwich.

Afternoon tours
City of London; river cruise to Hampton Court Palace or Windsor.

Evening tours
Romance of London including dinner cruise; escorted theme evenings.

Country Tours
Day tours
Leeds Castle; Stonehenge, Longleat and Bath; Stratford, Oxford, Bladon and the Cotswolds; Stratford and Warwick Castle; Boulogne.

Extended tours
Visit England's lovely cathedral cities and towns, Lake District, Stonehenge, Bath, Shakespeare country, Devon and Cornwall, Scotland, Wales and Ireland.

Tours pick up from most major hotels. For full details ask for a free leaflet at Travel Information Centres or phone 071-222 1234.

BEWARE OF PICKPOCKETS

Keep an eye on your money and credit cards in crowded areas. Men should know how foolish it is to put wallets in their back trouser pockets. Beware of being jostled in a queue as some pickpockets work in groups. Women should beware of bag snatchers. Thieves watch you withdraw cash then follow you discreetly. Sooner or later your attention slips and the bag disappears. Hook your bag handle round your ankle in restaurants and hang it on a hook in the Ladies if there is a gap under the door. Another villainous trick is to slice through shoulder bag straps with a razor-blade.

Always lock your car and hide valuables under the seat or in the boot (trunk). Don't drive with a handbag or camera on the passenger seat if the window is open. Enterprising thieves on bikes can hook them away and leave you fuming in the traffic.